CULTIVATING A PROPHETIC LIFESTYLE

LUC NIEBERGALL

Copyright © 2016 by Luc Niebergall

All rights reserved. This book or any portion thereof may not be reproduced or used in any manner whatsoever without the express written permission of the publisher except for the use of brief quotations in a book review.

Printed in the United States of America

First Edition, 2016

ISBN-10: 1537760424
ISBN-13: 978-1537760421

Royal Identity Ministries

Dedication

I dedicate this book to my friend Colette, for being the first person to ever see the calling over my life. Colette, thank you for being an inspiration to many, a mother of the faith, and for modelling what it looks like to be a friend of God.

Table of Content

New Testament Prophecy...9

Demystifying Prophecy..27

The Language of the Spirit...37

The Three Facets of Prophecy...................................55

Judging Prophetic Words...69

The Four Revelatory Gifts..77

Common Pitfalls of the Prophetic Ministry.............97

Friendship with God...115

Conclusion..125

As we make the decision to cultivate a personal culture of the prophetic, we are deciding to take on the heart and mind of Christ. The world tries to barricade our identities brick by brick, to mask the warmth of our inner beauty with cold and calloused stone. True prophetic people revel in potential, even if the natural eye is blind to its essence. They see past dysfunction into the vast fortress of undiscovered treasure. Prophecy sees through stone and calls forth castled destinies.

New Testament Prophecy

      I can still remember one of the first times I had ever received an accurate prophetic word from the Lord for someone.

      I was sitting in a restaurant sipping a cup of coffee, when suddenly my attention was drawn to a man who was a few tables down from me, writing in his journal. Immediately when I focused my attention on him, I saw in my mind's eye a picture of a small child running through a field trying to catch a butterfly. However, no matter how hard he tried, the butterfly was always just out of hand's grasp. I then heard the words subtly run through my mind, "I am about to open doors for this man that he has been

Cultivating A Prophetic Lifestyle

praying to have opened, and I am about to close doors that he has been praying to have closed.

Once I was able to build up enough confidence to approach the man with what I felt, I walked over to him and introduced myself.

Nervously, I said to him, "This might be kind of strange, but I am a Christian and I believe that God speaks today. I feel like I received a message for you. Do you mind if I share with you what I felt like the Lord said?"

The man nodded his approval, and motioned for me to continue.

I said, "I felt as though God said that ever since you were a child, you have felt like you have chased after beauty, yet it has always felt just out of hand's grasp. However, I feel like God is saying that He is about to open doors in your life that you have been praying would open, and He is about to close doors that you have prayed would close."

The man stared at me with a shocked look in his bewildered eyes. Sliding his journal across the table, he told me to read what he had just been writing moments before I approached him. The journal entry read:

New Testament Prophecy

"Dear God, ever since I was a small child, I have felt like I have been chasing beauty, yet it has been just out of hand's grasp. Open the doors that I have prayed would open for years now, and close the doors that I have prayed would close."

One of my greatest desires is to see the prophetic ministry restored to the church. I long to see God's children encounter the loving word of the Father in their lives. I believe that a true blessing from the Father can lead orphans into sonship and daughtership. Yet, in order for the world to receive the Father's blessing, the church needs to understand their supernatural access to the feelings of His heart. We then need to be equipped to be His mouthpiece on the earth.

My heart throughout this book is to give you clarity concerning how God speaks, so that you can encounter the Lord in friendship by hearing His voice. My heart is also that you would be equipped to speak His word wherever you are called. Revelation concerning our identity in Christ needs to push us into an understanding that we are the bridge for people's supernatural encounters with love. Love is not a concept meant to be merely talked about. Love is a person meant to be encountered.

There has been a lie in the church that many have embraced, which teaches that if we want to see a move of the Spirit, all we have to do is sit back and wait for God to move. In 1 Corinthians 14:1 we read

Cultivating A Prophetic Lifestyle

"Pursue love, and desire spiritual gifts, but especially that you may prophesy." When you translate the word "desire" in 1 Corinthians 14:1 from the Greek, it literally means to "lust after". So, this verse could actually be read: "Pursue love, and lust after spiritual gifts, but especially that you may prophesy."

When the apostle Paul wrote this to the Corinthians, he was not making a recommendation to the church. He was giving an apostolic commandment, saying that if the Corinthians wanted to see a sustained move of the Spirit, that they needed to seek and lust after the prophetic ministry. This verse debunks the false teaching which says that we need to "seek the Giver and not the gifts". We certainly need to seek the Giver first and foremost. However, in order for us to walk in power and to be vessels for freedom, we also need to seek the gifts of the Spirit, especially prophecy.

There is a lot of unnecessary mysticism and misunderstanding surrounding prophecy. This is incredibly unfortunate, yet understandable. It makes sense that the enemy would try and taint one of God's most valuable spiritual gifts. The enemy has tried to make the word of the Lord something to be feared; yet God is restoring this wonderful ministry to its rightful place. The prophetic ministry should only be feared if we have a distorted understanding of who the Father is. When we understand that the Father is loving and accepting, then we would be quick to embrace God's word through prophecy.

New Testament Prophecy

That being said, I am going to start off by confronting one of the greatest misconceptions concerning the prophetic ministry. I am doing this because it is necessary in order for me to build my teaching upon a proper foundation. Even though I am teaching more theologically at this point, make sure you are catching the heart of what I am writing.

In the 1980's, the global church experienced a swift acceleration of understanding concerning accessibility to the voice of the Lord through the cross. As people who are under the New Covenant, we examined the New Testament, looking for a prophetic leader to see how we should prophesy. Quickly, the emerging prophetic community discovered that there were not a vast amount of New Testament prophets in the Bible to study. In fact, the variety of those who were actually called prophets, other than Jesus, is minimal leaving us with only Agabus (Acts 21:10), Judas and Silas (Acts 15:32), of which there is very little mentioning. I also believe that John the Beloved operated as a prophet considering that he authored the book of Revelation; however, scripture does not call him a prophet by title. Since we did not see an embodiment of a prophetic figure in the New Testament after the cross and resurrection, we unfortunately dismissed Paul's teachings concerning this particular ministry in 1 Corinthians 14. We had a hungry group of people wanting to learn how to hear God's voice and speak His word. Since we did not see many prophets to refer to in the New Testament, the body of Christ looked where there was a vast variety of prophets; in the Old Testament.

The church began to use the Old Testament prophets as a template of how to prophesy. What happened when we did this, is that as New Testament people, we stepped into an Old Covenant mindset and began to prophesy under Old Testament principles. A primary function of a prophet's job in the Old Testament was to point out people's sin, since sin stood as a barrier between man and God. A bulk of their ministry was geared towards bringing correction, in hope that the people would repent and eliminate the sin in their lives that there may be reconciliation between man and God. If the people did not repent, it was then often a prophet's job to declare the repercussions of their stubbornness through condemnation and judgement. Since this was a common trait in Old Testament prophecy, many people in the 1980's began to prophesy from the standpoint of condemnation and judgement.

You can imagine how many people would have been hurt by this form of ministry. This is when it became popular for ministers to prophetically point out people's sin publicly in church meetings, which I never agree with or condone in any way. I do not believe that it is ever God's heart to humiliate His children. Since so many people were hurt by prophecy in the 1980's, many rejected it completely. Ever since this point in history, many in the church have been in a process of healing based on what happened due to

New Testament Prophecy

misconceptions concerning prophecy. In the present, mature prophets have been righting the wrongs of the past by working to create proper boundaries surrounding the prophetic, so that it can be a safe ministry to function in.

I believe that what Paul wrote in 1 Corinthians 14:3 is an excellent template for New Testament prophecy. It says, "He who prophesies speaks edification and exhortation and comfort to men."

Where Old Testament prophecy brought judgement and condemnation, New Testament prophecy brings "edification" which means to build up, "exhortation" which means to encourage, and comfort. We need to understand that the expression of prophecy has shifted because the covenant we live under has changed.

Look at the switch in the prophet Elijah's ministry between covenants. This is profound. Malachi 4:5-6 says, "Behold, I will send Elijah the prophet before the coming of the great and dreadful day of the Lord. And he will turn the hearts of the fathers to the children, and the hearts of the children to their fathers."

Church, this is important to grasp. In the Old Testament, Elijah's ministry consisted of slaying false prophets and calling down fire from heaven to consume people (1 Kings 18 and 2 Kings 1). In the New Testament, his prophetic ministry consists of reconciling families. See, Elijah's ministerial expression concerning prophecy completely changed because the covenant man lived under shifted.

If I were to simplify what prophecy is in New Testament times, it is to speak the heart of God and to declare what He Himself is already speaking. Prophecy reveals true kingdom identity. It calls forth calling and destiny. Our job as New Testament prophetic people is to look past people's dysfunctions, into the treasure of who they are. Our job is to see Jesus in people and to speak into the glory of who God has created them to be.

Scripture consistently teaches us that what we focus on we empower. Remember when Peter walked on water with Jesus? (Matthew 14:25-33). When Peter focused on Jesus he could walk on water, whereas when he focused on his circumstance, he empowered his circumstance. If we are continuously pointing people to their dysfunction as a method of prophesying, then we are empowering their dysfunction. On the other hand, if we point to who Jesus is in them, we empower Christ's work in them.

The world does a very good job of dehumanizing people, therefore veiling their greatness. History shows us a clear track record of the consistent tactic of dehumanization. The Holocaust was birthed through the dehumanization of Jewish people. Millions of Jews were killed because the Nazis looked through the lens of a lie, which kept Israel's greatness hidden. Abortion has barricaded the world from seeing the importance of human life. The lie of different classes between races brought discrimination, which led to racism and slavery. Still, every day, each person is confronted by dehumanization as lies threaten to hide our greatness.

New Testament prophecy looks past what the world assumes of us and calls forth what God has decreed over us. New Testament prophecy is not about pointing out our negative views about people; it is about declaring what their Father is already saying about them.

In Ezekiel 37, Ezekiel did not go around telling the dry bones that they were dry bones. He said, "Surely I will cause breath to enter into you, and you shall live. I will put sinews on you and bring flesh upon you, cover you with skin and put breath in you; and you shall live. Then you shall know that I am the LORD." Ezekiel spoke into their potential and the dry bones became a great army. Prophecy is releasing the heart of the Father over someone. If we are releasing the heart of the Father, then we need to understand that He sees His children through the lens of the blood of the Lamb.

When I was 20 years old, I was at a church service where God was moving powerfully. I sat under the teaching of a guest speaker who is a prophetic leader in the nations. As he taught, Holy Spirit spoke to me and said, "I just told the speaker to prophesy over you. This is what he is going to say to you: 'You have been faithful with the little, so God is going to give you much. As of today, you are being commissioned into ministry because you are called as a signpost to this generation.'"

After the Lord spoke this to me, I was sitting in the pew, questioning as to whether what I heard was the Lord or not. Not even two minutes passed, when the speaker instantly stopped mid-sentence and pointed at me. He said, "Stand up." Once I stood, he said, "You have been faithful with the little, so God is going to give you much. As of today, you are being commissioned into ministry because you are called as a signpost to this generation."

After the service, I was about to go home when Holy Spirit told me to go to a specific coffee shop in the city. When I arrived at the shop, I saw an old friend of mine who was having coffee with a friend of his. As we talked, he began to tell me that he and his friend were planting a house church together. We conversed, swapping stories of God moving and testimonies of healing. By the end of the conversation they invited me to speak at their church. This was the first offer I had ever received to speak at a church, and I received it within the same hour of receiving a prophetic word that I would be released into ministry that very day.

The night before I spoke at this church, I spent time waiting on the Lord. Holy Spirit began to give me words of knowledge for healing and showed me visions of some of the people who would be there. I waited a while longer, when I suddenly saw a vision of God sitting on His throne. Hanging from His neck was a necklace with a heart shaped locket. I asked God why He wore a heart shaped locket. Upon waiting for an answer, I felt like He shared with me that the locket was the nation of Israel and that I was going to prophetically commission a woman at the service, because she was called to be a missionary to Israel. He went on to say that she would bring incredible change in that particular nation because her heart would break for what the Lord's heart breaks for.

I asked the Lord how I would know who the woman was, and He responded with an answer that I did not understand at the time. He said, "she will be drawn to the necklace."

I arrived at the house church Sunday morning. Before the meeting began, I sat down on one of the couches and began to spend time with Holy Spirit. As I conversed with God, I watched as a young-five-year-old girl ran around the living room playing. The door suddenly opened when a woman walked in wearing a very large necklace. Remembering my vision from the night before, I was intently watching the circumstance unfold. I watched as the young-five-year-old girl ran up to the woman shouting, "I love your necklace! I love your necklace!"

Instantly the words rang through my head, "She will be drawn to the necklace." The realization struck me that this young-five-year-old girl was called to be the nation changing missionary to Israel. I instantly was moved and began to weep.

As I spoke during the service, I called up the girl and her father and mother. All three were crying as the Lord spoke destiny into the young girl through a prophetic word.

The reason why I shared this particular story is because I believe it is an excellent example concerning what true prophecy is. Our job as prophetic people is to look past the enemy's accusations toward God's children. It is to look past what the world sees and to call forth what God sees. The world saw a five-year-old girl. God saw a nation changer.

Correctional Prophecy

Often people will ask me what my thoughts are on correctional prophetic ministry in New Testament times. I do believe that there are times for correctional prophecy, however I believe that these types of words should be done with both order and integrity. These types of words function well in the context of relationship. What I mean by this is, since my wife and I are in relationship, I have given her permission to speak into my life if she notices that something in my heart or ministry should change. It is our relationship that gives her this right in my life. I also have an accountability team for my ministry and different friends who I have given this level of trust to. I also think that correctional prophetic ministry is fine if you are a leader and you need to bring order into someone's life who you have been entrusted to lead. This of course should not be done publicly, but can be done in more of a private and honouring manner. The same could be said if you are intentionally discipling someone, and they have given you permission to bring correction to their life. I also know some proven prophets in the world who will receive the rare correctional word for someone, but they wield these words with integrity. First off, they do not give them publicly, and they have an accountability team around them who can help judge these more controversial types of words.

I hope you understand my heart in what I am saying. I am not trying to say that God will never give correctional words. God can speak however He chooses. However, my heart is to place up proper boundaries within this ministry so that people are protected from feeling as though prophecy is an invasive and exposing ministry.

Cultivating A Prophetic Lifestyle

The Power of the Tongue

I believe a pivotal revelation pertaining to reigning as royalty, is having an understanding of the prophetic ministry. I believe this because since we are kings and queens in God's kingdom in our land of influence, it is necessary for us to understand the importance of a king and queen's decree. When a royal authority speaks within the land which has been given to them, whatever they decree is established. When you carry authority, which you do as co-heirs with Christ, your words carry tremendous weight.

Proverbs 18:21: "Death and life are in the power of the tongue, and those who love it will eat its fruit."

Job 22:28: "You will also declare a thing, and it will be established for you; so light will shine on your ways."

Numbers 14:28: "Say to them, 'As I live,' says the LORD, 'just as you have spoken in My hearing, so I will do to you.'"

1 Samuel 1 tells a story of a man named Elkanah. Elkanah had two wives whose names were Hannah and Peninnah. Peninnah bore children for Elkanah whereas Hannah was barren. Hannah would

go to the house of the Lord once a year to worship God. One time as she worshiped, she wept in anguish because of her barrenness. She made a vow and said, "O LORD of hosts, if You will indeed look on the affliction of Your maidservant and remember me, and not forget Your maidservant, but will give Your maidservant a male child, then I will give him to the LORD all the days of his life, and no razor shall come upon his head" (1 Samuel 1:11).

The priest Eli noticed her weeping and blessed her saying, "Go in peace, and the God of Israel grant your petition which you have asked of Him" (1 Samuel 1:17).

It came to pass that Hannah conceived a child and named him Samuel. Samuel's life, and his entire ministry was the fruit of the priest Eli's declaration of life.

A public school teacher that I know once taught his students about the power of the tongue. He kept a plant at the front of his desk. This man would not give the plant any water or sunlight. The plant would of course wither and die. Once the plant was dead, to start off each class, he and his students would then declare that the plant would live. On the third day, the plant came back to life simply through declaration. They killed and raised this plant from the dead in the total of five times simply through declaration. What an incredible lesson this would have been for those students concerning the power of the tongue.

All of creation was brought into existence through prophetic declaration. God did not think "let there be light" and there was light. He spoke it, and light manifested. Since we are kings and queens who were created in the direct image of the all-powerful God, our declarations carry tremendous power (Revelation 1:6).

When we use prophecy as a tool to judge and condemn, it is no wonder why people continue living in dysfunction. It is important for us to allow our tongue to be bound to the heart of God. This way, instead of being administrators of death, we become co-creators with God to create life with Him. The truth is that we need to be filled with such love to the extent where we are willing to speak life instead of death over people.

Unfortunately, the accuser of the brethren has been using the saints as a vessel to accuse the brethren. We need to allow the family of God to become a safe place where the accuser has no voice within community, only edification, exhortation and comfort. While teaching training and equipping schools concerning the prophetic ministry, I get the great privilege of seeing God change the hearts of people who would use prophecy as a tool to accuse and judge, to being vessels of love from the Father's heart.

New Testament Prophecy

To end off this chapter, I want you to take the time right now to pray this prayer with me:

"*Lord, forgive me for any time that I may have spoken any form of death over anyone, including myself. I make the decision right now to change the way I think concerning prophecy. I choose to prophesy from a New Testament perspective. I make the decision to speak life instead of death. Use me to be a vessel of love by binding my tongue to your heart, Lord.*"

Demystifying Prophecy

Inspirational Prophecy

Hearing the voice of God has the reputation of being mystical, when really, prophecy is supposed to be an incredibly normal and common aspect of life for believers. In order to move in the prophetic ministry, you do not have to be mystical. You can actually be yourself, because hearing God's voice should be common for every believer.

Inspirational prophecy is the concept that every believer can prophesy because of what was accomplished at the cross. Prophecy is not reserved for prophets as it was in the Old Testament. Through the cross, we were all brought into direct relationship with God, permitting us to continually converse with Him.

Learning to prophesy is much like turning on a switch. It is not about striving. Giving prophetic words is not what makes you prophetic, because you are already prophetic in your DNA as a Christian. You are already prophetic because the cross brought you into a relationship with God, who loves to speak to you. We can turn on the switch by simply stepping into this often overlooked aspect of our identity.

I will be the first to confess that I had great difficulty when I first began to move in the prophetic ministry. After I first met Jesus, I became obsessed with hearing His voice. On Saturday nights when all of my friends would be out partying or playing video games, I would be out walking with God for hours at a time practicing hearing His voice. On my walks, I would ask God for prophetic words for people I knew. With my pen poised above my notebook, I would wait. Usually it would take me about a half an hour to get a word, and my word would be as elaborate as "Jesus loves you".

Although my prophetic words were vague, God saw someone who was hungry for His word. He saw someone who was faithful with the little, so therefore He could give much. Now, if I am in a room full of people, I can give every individual a specific and detailed prophetic word about their life. God honours our hunger by satisfying it. When we are faithful with the little, He gives us much.

Acts 2:17: "And it shall come to pass in the last days, says God, That I will pour out of My Spirit on all flesh; Your sons and your daughters shall prophesy, Your young men shall see visions, Your old men shall dream dreams."

This is so good. The words "all flesh" in this verse are translated from the Greek as "whole body". This verse is saying that the whole church has accessibility to the voice of God. Who does it say that will prophesy? Sons and daughters. The sons and daughters of the living God will prophesy.

In John 10:27 Jesus says, "My sheep hear My voice, and I know them, and they follow Me." If you know Jesus as your shepherd, then He is continually speaking to you.

In Luke 4:4 Jesus said, "Man shall not live by bread alone, but by every word of God." In the Greek language there are two words for "word". There is the *logos* word, which means "written word". This is referring to scripture. There is also the *rhema* word, which means "spoken word" which is the prophetic word. In this verse when Jesus said that man lives on every word of God, the word, "word" that Jesus used here is referring to the *rhema* word. Man shall not live by bread alone, but by the spoken word of God.

This is excellent news! No matter who you are in the body of Christ, God's heart is to speak to you because you are His child. There has been a lie in the church that says only prophets can prophesy. However, the Bible clearly tells us that through the cross we were all brought into a communicable relationship with God.

In the next chapter we will take a look at the different ways God speaks and how we can tune our ears to hear what He is saying.

The Ministry of Prophecy

While every believer can prophesy, there are some who function in what I call the ministry of prophecy. I consider those who move in a ministry of prophecy, people who have allowed their prophetic gift to grow into a place of maturity. One of the characteristics of someone who has a ministry of prophecy is that one of their primary facets of ministry will be functioning prophetically. They will be those trusted by leadership to take care of greater prophetic matters in the church.

The Office of a Prophet

Ephesians 4:11-12: "And He Himself gave some to be apostles, some prophets, some evangelists, and some pastors and teachers, for the equipping of the saints for the work of ministry, for the edifying of the body of Christ."

We need to understand that where scripture tells us that every believer can prophesy, not everyone who prophesies is a prophet. Prophets play a big role in the church to hear and declare God's word, but one of their main functions is to train and equip the church to do what comes natural to them, which is to hear God's voice. This is one of the things that separates a prophet from prophetic people or someone who has a ministry of prophecy. Prophetic people prophesy, whereas prophets not only prophesy, they train people in how to prophesy as well. Since prophets have a grace over their lives to see and hear what God is doing, one of their functions in ministry is to equip others to do the same.

The desire of a prophet should be that those he or she trains would go further then they themselves do. This is important because the people of the church are the ones who are strategically placed in the marketplace to speak the word of the Lord. Prophets doing their job to train and equip the saints for ministry actually extends the word of the Lord from the church into the realms of business, government, education, arts, entertainment, media and families.

Prophets not doing their job to train and equip, creates an unhealthy dependency between the saints and prophets to hear the word of God for them. This means that prophets are ordained by God to demystify prophecy, visions, dreams, angelic visitations and prophetic encounters, showing their accessibility to every believer. Prophets are the ones who are commissioned by the Lord to put up the proper boundaries to transition the prophetic ministry out of infancy and into adulthood.

Prophets will carry what I call "the spirit of prophecy". Look at this:

1 Samuel 10:10-11: "There was a group of prophets to meet him (Saul); then the Spirit of God came upon him Saul, and he prophesied among them. And it happened, when all who knew him formerly saw that he indeed prophesied among the prophets, that the people said to one another, 'What is this that has come upon the son of Kish? Is Saul also among the prophets?'"

Prophets carry a sphere of authority where, when people are around them there is a grace to tap into what comes natural to them. While being around or under a prophet's anointing, people will often experience an increase in the accuracy concerning their prophetic words. They will also often experience an increase in visions, dreams and prophetic encounters.

While people who move in a gift of prophecy may speak into the lives of many people, prophets will often have favour to speak into the ears of those with great influence. If you look in the Old Testament, we can see that prophets had the ears of kings and government leaders to speak to. They would often give direction to entire nations concerning a nation's direction. The same can be said for prophets today. Prophets may have influence to prophesy the word of the Lord to government leaders, significant business leaders, celebrities or church leaders. In the New Testament, we can see that the prophet Agabus had the ear of Paul the Apostle, who was probably the greatest apostle who ever lived, other than Jesus (Acts 21:10-11).

Prophetic Exercise

In the last two chapters, we have learned what it looks like to perceive the prophetic ministry through a New Testament lens and that hearing God's voice is for everyone. Now what we are going to do is activate what we have learned.

This is very important. You could listen to dozens of teachings on prophecy, and read a multitude of books on the topic, however, you will not learn to hear the voice of God unless you begin to take time to listen to what He has to say. It is not enough to simply receive teaching in your heart; we need to water those seeds of revelation so that they become our own personal truths.

Before we learn to hear God speak for others, I want to walk you through an exercise to learn to hear God's voice for yourself. Remember that as we do this exercise, God is only going to speak things that build you up, encourage, and comfort you (1 Corinthians 14:3). He is not going to tear you down or speak anything negative into you. God simply wants to affirm you as His child.

What I want you to do right now is position yourself in a posture to receive from God. Still your heart and mind before Him.

Demystifying Prophecy

I am going to lead you through a series of questions for you to ask God. Remember that Holy Spirit is an internal God, so therefore you may not hear an audible voice; but would more likely hear Him from the still small voice inside your heart and mind. You may even see pictures in your mind's eye as a way of God speaking to you.

When you are ready, ask the Lord this question:

"God, if you were to play a game with me, what game would you play?"

Once you feel God answer, then ask Him this:

"How does this game apply to my life?"

Now I want you to ask the Lord this:

"God, what do you think of me? What words of encouragement do you want to speak into my life right now?"

Cultivating A Prophetic Lifestyle

As you begin to hear God speak, I would encourage you to write down anything you felt the Lord speak into your life. This helps us to remember what God has declared over us, and is a good posture in stewarding the spoken word of God.

The Language of the Spirit

1 Samuel 3 tells us a story of Samuel in his pre-prophet years. One time while Samuel was laying by the ark of God, the Lord called his name audibly. When Samuel heard his name being called, he misinterpreted it for his mentor, Eli's voice. Samuel got up and said to Eli, "Here I am, for you called me."

Eli told Samuel that he did not call his name and told him to lay back down. When Samuel laid down, the Lord called him again by name. Samuel again went to Eli to receive the same response.

God called him a third time, except this time when Samuel went to Eli, Eli recognized that this was God speaking to Samuel. Eli said to Samuel, "Go, lie down; and it shall be, if He calls you, that you must say, 'Speak, Lord, for Your servant hears.'"

The fourth time Samuel laid down, God called to Samuel, and he responded saying, "Speak, for Your servant hears."

Samuel in his pre-prophet years was caught in an audible voice encounter with the Lord. However, since he did not understand how God spoke, he did not even know that it was God speaking. We have previously looked at scripture to see that God speaks to every believer. Even though He is speaking, we often do not understand how to discern His voice because we do not understand the language of the Spirit.

We are going to look at the different ways throughout scripture that God will speak to His people to gain clarity. Keep in mind that God is not limited to speak in only these ways. He can speak however He chooses.

The Written Word of God

Hebrews 4:12: "For the word of God is living and powerful, and sharper than any two-edged sword, piercing even to the division of soul and spirit, and of joints and marrow, and is a discerner of the thoughts and intents of the heart."

The Greek word for "word" in this verse is *logos,* which is referring to the written Word of God. God's Word is living and active! It is good news that the Bible is not a dead word. It is alive because it is God-breathed. Every word and verse in the Bible is an open heaven for us to come into a revelatory encounter with Jesus. As Holy Spirit teaches us through His written Word, the *logos* word becomes *rhema* to us.

I believe that if we are ever to come to a place of maturity in speaking the Now Prophetic word (*rhema*), we need to be rooted in the written Word. In Revelation 1:16, John has an encounter where He sees Jesus in heavenly form, and out of Jesus' mouth was a double-edged sword. Every one of us needs to be completely rooted in the *logos* word, and engulfed in the *rhema* word, thus operating as the double edged sword. As prophetic people we will never be able to properly discern God's voice if we are not deeply rooted in the scriptures.

The Still Small Voice

1 Kings 19:11-13: "It (God's presence) wasn't in the wind, earthquake, or fire, but in the still small voice that the Lord spoke to Elijah."

Cultivating A Prophetic Lifestyle

Even though this might seem like the least extreme or supernatural way to hear God speak, I believe that it is the most common. Some people think that if God wants to speak, that He will speak audibly in order to get His point across. Although He may do this, I believe we are a people who God wants to be so close with that we will hear His gentle whisper. Since Holy Spirit is an internal God, He will use things such as our thought process and impressions to communicate. When we walk intimately with the Lord, our ears are tuned to discern Holy Spirit's voice from your own thoughts.

A lot of times when God gives me specific words of knowledge for meetings where I minister, I often receive them when I spend time with Him in the secret place in preparation to speak. God does not often speak to me audibly or send an angel to tell me things such as, "There will be a woman at the meeting you will be speaking at who has a cancerous jump under the right side of her rib cage." Where God can speak audibly or through angels, these specific words of knowledge will usually come through a spontaneous God thought and I have to receive the word by faith.

A lot of the time when we receive prophetic words through the still small voice of God, it will come as a thought. What we need to do is learn to pull on that small thought until it becomes a prophetic word.

The Language of the Spirit

One time when I was walking around a book store, I saw a man sitting down by himself. I felt like Holy Spirit was prompting me to talk to him. I went up to him and said, "I believe that God speaks today, and I feel like He has a word for you."

At this point, I actually did not even have a word to give him. I was just stepping out in faith, believing that God would show up. Suddenly the word "son" popped into my head. I started speaking out what God gave me and began to pull a word right out of the Father's heart for him.

I said to the man, "I feel like God just told me that you have two sons, and that for the past two weeks you have been lying awake in bed at night, daydreaming about having more of an emotional connection with your youngest son. I feel like God is saying that you are going to notice a drastic change in how your son connects with you in these next three months."

The man had tears in his eyes and told me that everything I said was true.

I then felt like God said to me that this man had a desire in his heart to start a business. So I pulled on the word and said, "I feel like God is saying that you have a business anointing over your life and that you have tried to start several businesses in the past 15 years, but they did not turn out the way that you wanted them to. You feel frustrated and stuck now because you did not see the desire of your heart come to pass."

I then said, "You are wanting to start a construction business in fine carpentry, aren't you?" He nodded his head, shocked. I said to him, "In these next six months, you are going to meet two Christian men who are going to want to help you start up your business. I feel like God is saying that you can trust them because He trusts them."

Notice how this was an incredibly detailed word that I gave this man about his life, yet it did not come through an audible voice from God. God spoke through my thought process. Most prophets or well-known prophetic leaders that I know receive their most specific words through the still small voice of God. We need to be a people who will allow God to fine tune our ears to hear the word of the Lord, even if He is speaking in His faintest whisper.

Visions

Numbers 12:6-8: "Then He said, 'Hear now My words: If there is a prophet among you, I the Lord, make Myself known to Him in a vision; I speak to Him in a dream, not so with my servant Moses; He is faithful in all My house. I speak with Him face to face, even plainly and not in dark sayings; and he sees the form of the Lord. Why then are you not afraid to speak against My servant Moses?'"

There are a few different visions that God will use to speak to us:

Mind's eye vision:

A mind's eye vision is when God will show you a picture or a movie on the screen of your mind. A lot of people think that in order for a vision to be legitimate, that your sight needs to black out and you have to see what God wants to show you with your natural eyes. This is not true. Daniel 7:15 tells us that Daniel was troubled by the visions in his head, telling us that the realm of visions is in the mind. Even a gentle picture in your mind's eye can be a vision from the Lord.

Closed eye vision:

A closed eye vision is where God will open your "spiritual eyes" to the spiritual realm. This means that you are not seeing spiritual things with your natural eyes as clearly as you and I may be able to see each other, but are seeing in the spirit by faith.

Cultivating A Prophetic Lifestyle

Open vision:

An open vision is where God will open your natural eyes to see spiritual things clearly.

2 Kings 6:16-17: "So he answered, 'Do not fear, for those who are with us are more than those who are with them.' And Elisha prayed, and said, 'LORD, I pray, open his eyes that he may see.' Then the LORD opened the eyes of the young man, and he saw. And behold, the mountain was full of horses and chariots of fire all around Elisha."

Here are some other examples from the Bible where visions are discussed:

Acts 16:9-10	Hosea 12:10
Daniel 2:28	Daniel 7:15
Jeremiah 1:11	Acts 7:55-56
Ezekiel 1:1	Ezekiel 8:3
Acts 26:19	

Dreams

Dreams are a very common language that God uses to communicate. However, not every dream we have is from God. Some dreams are from God, some are from the enemy, and others are because we had pizza before we went to bed. All throughout scripture we can see that dreams and dream interpretation are common ways that God speaks.

In the secular world, Sigmund Freud was the pioneer of the theory that dreams are an expression of our inner man communicating with the mind. He taught that we subconsciously tell ourselves through dreams if we have problems or issues that need to be resolved. The Bible teaches that our dream lives are an avenue for God to speak to us.

The Hebrew word for "dream" means to "bind firmly". When we have a dream from the Lord, it is because He is trying to bind a message firmly to our heart. Joseph held onto his dream for over 20 years and it came to pass. The promise that he received in his dream actually sustained him through his time of trials.

Symbolism is incredibly important while interpreting dreams, because while some dreams are literal, most are made up of symbols. Things such as colours and numbers are important to understand while interpreting dreams. The greatest key I can give you concerning interpreting dreams is to learn how Holy Spirit speaks. Since we all live unique lives, a symbol might mean something different depending on the person. I mean this in the sense that, when I see a horse in a dream, to me it is usually symbolic of a movement of the Spirit of God. Whereas if someone else sees a horse, to them it might symbolize their past if they grew up on a farm. So, the best way to learn to interpret dreams properly is to learn how Holy Spirit speaks. This way we are not attempting to create a system for dream interpretation. If we are trying to interpret dreams apart from Holy Spirit, we will end up with fleshy interpretations.

Genesis 40:8: "And they said to him (Joseph), 'We each have had a dream, and there is no interpreter of it.' So Joseph said to them, 'Do not interpretations belong to God? Tell them to me, please.'"

A great exercise to increase your dream life is to keep a notebook beside your bed to record what you dream. Your dream life can increase through this because you are stepping out in faith by allowing your expectation to rise, believing that the Lord will speak to you in the night season. When we are intentionally recording our dreams, we are proving ourselves as good stewards of God's word. I know of many individuals who have practiced doing this, and have seen a drastic increase in their dream lives.

The Audible Voice of God

John 12:28: "Then a voice came from heaven, saying, 'I have both glorified it and will glorify it again.'"

The audible voice of God is when God will speak audibly instead of with the still small voice. Although I know many seasoned prophets who have heard God's audible voice, this is not usually the most common way for God to speak to them. Even seasoned prophets typically hear from God most often through His still small voice, as well as through visions and dreams. I myself have heard the Lord speak audibly many times, but it also is not the most frequent way that God speaks to me.

Trances

Acts 11:5: "I was in the city of Joppa praying, and in a trance I saw a vision, an object descending like a great sheet, let down from heaven by four corners;

Cultivating A Prophetic Lifestyle

and it came to me."

Trance may sound like a word used in New Age practices, but scripture proves that this is a way that God speaks today. The enemy cannot create, but he will attempt to steal what God has already created to try and pervert it. It is time that we claim back what God has created for His children.

The word "trance" translated to Greek is *extasis* which is from the word *existemi*, which literally means "ecstasy". The definition of ecstasy is: Displacing an individual's state of mind with an elevated God given state for the purpose of instructing him

In Acts 11:5, it says that when Peter was in a trance, he saw a vision. A trance is a state of raised awareness that we can fall into so that we can clearly hear what Holy Spirit is speaking to us. Trances are actually a very common thing, which you may have already experienced without even realizing it. I am just going to add terminology and show you the significance to spiritual experiences which are often overlooked. Do you know that feeling when you are in between wakefulness and asleep? Your mind starts showing you things that you would never have thought of when you were awake. Not every time, but I believe that a lot of the time, this is a trance.

Here is another example of a trance: While you have been worshipping, have you ever felt so consumed with the Lord's presence that you could not

The Language of the Spirit

take your focus from Him even if you tried? If so, then you have experienced a trance. In these moments, you are in an enhanced awareness of what God is doing and saying. This is a trance from the Lord.

God speaks through avenues such as dreams, visions and trances because they bypass our intellect and logic so that we do not reason ourselves out of hearing God's word.

Numbers 24:4: "He hath said, which heard the words of God, which saw the vision of the Almighty, falling into a trance, but having his eyes open." (KJV)

Community

As prophetic people, we will at times have the faith to believe that God can speak to us in the most supernatural ways. We will believe that God can speak through heavenly experiences, fire falling from the sky and through signs and wonders. Yet, we often overlook one of the most common ways that God wants to speak to His children; through close and transparent relationships.

Cultivating A Prophetic Lifestyle

I have met numerous prophetic people who will say things to me like, "A few years ago I could hear God crystal clear, but then I entered a season where His voice seemed dimmed. I thought this would only happen for a short amount of time, but this has now been going on for years."

There are a variety of different reasons why God's voice may seem dimmed to us. However, I have noticed that often when there seems to be an immediate disconnect like this, that God is still actually speaking, He is just trying to speak to us in a way that we are unfamiliar with in hearing Him. He is trying to broaden our capacity to receive His word. Often prophetic people will slip into these forms of seasons because God is actually trying to teach them how to hear Him through community. However, when we make the decision to not hear in this way, it comes across as God being silent.

God's heart is for everyone to be woven into His family and to be in transparent relationships. All throughout scripture we can see that God's heart is for relationships and that people are a common vessel for Him to speak through.

Angels

Acts 8:26: "Now an angel of the Lord spoke to Phillip, saying, 'Arise and go toward the south along the road which is going down from Jerusalem to Gaza.'"

Some people get uncomfortable when I talk about angels, but the truth is that God still uses angels to speak and minister to people. Angels are a part of God's kingdom. We do not get uncomfortable with teachings concerning other aspects of God's kingdom such as peace and joy, so we should not be offended by the angelic. Hebrews 1:14 says, "Are they not all ministering spirits sent forth to minister to those who will inherit salvation?"

There are numerous accounts of angels in the Bible, most of which involved interactions with mankind. In many instances, when there was a profound thing taking place in scripture, angels were mentioned.

I am a firm believer that as believers we can experience the spirit realm. I will share a story with you to give you some context as to what an angelic encounter could look like.

A couple of years ago, I was going through a very difficult season in my life. This was a season where I was experiencing much discouragement concerning what I was called to in ministry, and different circumstances were forcefully pressing against me causing much anxiety.

I remember one evening while I was lying in bed about to go to sleep, I asked the Lord for help and for grace to stand strong in the season that I was going through at the time. As I was attempting to fall asleep, I saw something in my peripheral vision. Looking over, I saw what looked like a short man wearing a light blue robe. The man looked like he was in his late 20's in age. In his hands, he was holding out a book looking as though he was reading. Holy Spirit then spoke to me saying, "I have sent this angel to you to minister to you while you sleep, by reading the declarations of the Lord over you."

This same night I had a very profound dream from the heart of the Lord, which marked a shift in season for my life. This angelic encounter launched me down a road that led me out from my discouragement and ushered me into a time of stepping into much greater influence in my calling.

While things such as angelic encounters may seem out of our boxes, we need to take a posture of humility to invite the Lord to minister to us in whatever way He chooses.

Prophetic Encounters

Prophetic encounters are a way that God still speaks today. Some of these encounters involve out-of-body experiences (2 Kings 5:26), being transported (Acts 8:26-40), signs and wonders, third-heaven encounters (Ezekiel 1, Isaiah 6, 2 Corinthians 12:1-3), and visitations from the Lord Himself (Acts 9, Revelation 1).

Conclusion

Sometimes we limit our ability to hear the Lord based on how we expect Him to speak. The truth is that God can speak in any way He wants, and if we pick and choose how we think He should speak, we might just miss the word of the Lord.

Remember in John 12 when Jesus was teaching parables to a group of people? In verses 28 and 29 Jesus says, "'Father, glorify Your name.' Then a voice came from heaven, saying, 'I have both glorified it and will glorify it again.' Therefore, the people who stood by and heard it said that it had thundered. Others said, 'An angel has spoken to Him.'"

Cultivating A Prophetic Lifestyle

We need to catch this. A voice came down from heaven and spoke audibly, but only some heard a voice whereas others heard thunder. What was the difference between those who heard the voice and those who heard thunder? Some had positioned their hearts to hear the word of the Lord in whichever way God chose to speak, whereas others did not.

We need to be open to the Lord speaking to us in whichever way He chooses. Two key reasons why we do not encounter the Lord in different and abstract ways is, first of all, because we do not expect it. Second of all, is often because we choose not to ask Him.

I would encourage you to go through the list of ways that God speaks, and to ask Holy Spirit to open your expectancy to receive His word through each. As you ask Him, allow expectancy to build in your heart that the Lord wants to speak to you. A lot of the time, we will say the prayers but in our hearts we believe that we are not worthy of such experiences. We believe that our friends or family will receive the blessings before we ourselves do. The truth is that you are God's favourite. He chose you and He longs for you to hear His voice.

The Three Facets of Prophecy

There are three facets of prophecy. There is receiving the word, interpreting the word and delivering the word. Learning how to function in all three is essential for speaking the word of God. We are going to walk through each together to learn how to properly flow in the prophetic ministry.

Receiving The Word

The first facet of prophecy is receiving the word. It is actually incredibly simple to receive a word for

Cultivating A Prophetic Lifestyle

someone. Psalm 139:17-18 says, "How precious also are Your thoughts to me, O God! How great is the sum of them! If I should count them, they would be more in number than the sand."

The truth of the matter is that God has limitless good thoughts towards each person. His thoughts towards us are so endless that they outweigh the grains of sand. All that you need to do to encourage someone with a prophetic word is to tap into one of those thoughts.

I want to clarify something very important to break some unnecessary tension before we start. If you receive or speak a prophetic word with a good heart, and your word is not 100% correct, that does not mean you are a false prophet. It means that you are learning. I say this because I want you to know that there is grace for mistakes as you are learning to hear the voice of God.

One of the most common questions I am asked when I train and equip people in the prophetic ministry is how to tell the difference between God's voice and our own thoughts. This is a very valid question considering that there are different influences from the spirit realm that we can hear. We need to learn to distinguish the difference between the voice of Holy Spirit, the voice of our own spirit and mind, and sometimes demonic and angelic spirits. I am going to give you some tips regarding how to receive a word

The Three Facets of Prophecy

and to discern whether or not it is the voice of the Lord.

- Your first step is to wait on the Lord.

What is it that you are seeing and hearing? When you are receiving a prophetic word from the Lord for someone, the word will often come through the still small voice or a vision in the mind's eye. This is not always the case, but as I have mentioned earlier, these are often the most common ways for God to deposit prophetic messages.

- Remember, your prophetic word should always edify, exhort and comfort.

Sometimes when people start off learning to prophesy, they will see more of the negative than the positive in people. While we may at times see the negative with our discernment, this should not prevent us from seeing the good and the potential in people. Remember, to be truly prophetic is to see past dysfunction and assumption into who the person was created to be.

For some, when they first begin to receive visions for people will see negative pictures instead of uplifting one's, even though their heart is to build people up. This can sometimes occur because the visionary lens has been tainted. Sometimes when people have grown up watching things like pornography or horror movies they will have a tainted visionary lens because they have been more prone to seeing negative things. If you have noticed this pattern while trying to prophesy, then simply ask the Lord to cleanse your visionary lens. God will begin to re-pattern how you see.

- Does the word that you are receiving line up with the Bible?

We need to always remember that the prophetic word of God will always submit to the written word of God. I have met some who believe otherwise, however, everything we feel that we hear the Lord say should be supported by scripture.

- Usually when I am developing a prophetic community, I set a standard rule that there should be no prophesying concerning dates, mates or babies. What I mean by this, is that we should not be prophesying concerning who people will marry, who they should date, or timelines for having children.

The Three Facets of Prophecy

The reason being, is that there are just some things that are too close to the heart to practice giving prophetic words about. We are all students, still learning and growing in our ability to hear God's voice. With more tender topics such as these, I believe God would more so want to speak to us personally about them, considering we are all capable of making mistakes.

- Do not try to use someone's physical appearance as a template to receive a word for them.

When Samuel was about to anoint David as king over Israel in 1 Samuel 16, God says to him in verse 7, "Do not look at his appearance or at his physical stature, because I have refused him. For the LORD does not see as man sees; for man looks at the outward appearance, but the LORD looks at the heart." Samuel was a highly mature prophet, yet God found it necessary to remind him of this.

I have always found Samson an interesting person in the Bible. Samson was the strongest man recorded in scripture, yet his size or muscles were never mentioned even once. Goliath's appearance and size were described in great detail, so considering how Samson had a greater reputation concerning strength, you would assume that something about his size would have been mentioned. I believe that the reason why his size was not mentioned was because Samson was probably a regular man in size. The truth is that God hides greatness in human vessels. As prophetic people it is our job to see through one another's humanity and normality to see the essence of Christ's divinity.

- Do not have pre-assumptions of what God will speak.

There is a temptation in the prophetic ministry to believe that the most specific words are the most impactful. We really need to understand that God's word is not anointed because it is specific. It is anointed because God said it.

When God taught me this lesson I was ministering abroad. One day on my ministry trip, Holy Spirit spoke to me saying, "In two days, you are going to meet a man who has a broken bone in his right hand, right beneath his pinkie finger."

I was excited because this word was pretty specific so I knew that whoever this man was, he was going to get rocked by the love of God.

Two days later, I was walking downtown with a group of about 20 people. We were walking past a busker who was playing guitar and singing. When the man saw me, he stopped playing in mid-song, pointed

The Three Facets of Prophecy

at me and said, "You! Get over here!"

Not fully understanding what was going on, I walked over to him and went to shake his hand to introduce myself. The man stopped me saying, "I can't shake your hand. I punched a wall yesterday and broke a bone doing so."

I said to him, "You broke the bone right under your pinkie didn't you?"

Responding he said, "Yes, how did you know?"

I told the man, "Well, I'm a Christian and God spoke to me and told me that I was going to meet a man who broke a bone in his right hand, below his pinkie. If you let me pray for you then God will heal your hand."

"I don't want your prayer!" the man shouted at me.

I was a little caught off guard since the specific word of knowledge had no effect on him. Holy Spirit then spoke to me saying, "Since the specific word of knowledge did not work, tell him that he is a good man and that I love his heart."

I looked this man in the eyes and said to him, "You know, you are a good man and God really loves your heart."

Instantly this hard man broke down sobbing and gave his heart to Jesus.

The power of God's word is amazing to me. As prophetic people we really need to learn to heed this lesson. God's word is not anointed because it is specific. It is anointed because God said it.

Isaiah 50:4: "The Lord GOD has given Me the tongue of the learned, that I should know how to speak a word in season to him who is weary. He awakens Me morning by morning; He awakens My ear to hear as the learned."

We can actually develop our ears to hear the exact thoughts of the Lord, to speak a word in season. In this instance, reading this man's mail prophetically was not what unlocked his heart to the Lord; it was a word in season.

Interpreting The Word

The second facet of prophecy is interpreting the word. Interpretation is usually only necessary when God speaks through visions. When God gives you a picture vision in your mind for someone and you do not know what it means, then ask Holy Spirit. Holy Spirit may give you the interpretation, or He may not. Sometimes God will not reveal the interpretation to the person prophesying because the message is something intimate between God and the recipient of the word. If He does not give you an interpretation, then just share what the Lord showed you, instead of trying to fabricate an interpretation.

A friend of mine told me a story a long time ago. One time, while she was conducting an inner healing session with a woman, she was waiting upon the Lord. All of a sudden she received a very simple vision in her mind's eye. It was a vision of a rubber ducky. She went on to ask Holy Spirit for an interpretation for the bizarre vision. Holy Spirit went on to tell her that this picture was a personal word between Him and the woman, so He did not want to give the interpretation to her.

My friend then shared with the woman the vision of the rubber ducky, which resulted in the woman sobbing in tears. This simple vision actually was a very pivotal key to this woman receiving profound inner healing in her heart.

Delivering The Word

Delivering prophetic words with integrity is incredibly important, because a perfectly good prophetic word can be ruined by a poor delivery. Remember Joseph's dream in Genesis 37:5-8? Joseph had a word from God, but his delivery did not come across very well, so therefore he created a mess for himself with those he shared it with.

Here are some tips in how to deliver a word properly:

- Let your attitude, tone, and character line up with the focus of the word God is speaking. Let your spirit, attitude, tone and character represent Christ when you are delivering the word. When you give a word you do not have to raise your voice in order for the word to be anointed. The word will be anointed because God said it.

- When you deliver a word, you do not have to speak in Old English saying, "thus saith the Lord". Take the approach of saying, "I feel like the Lord is saying…." This way it diminishes

The Three Facets of Prophecy

unnecessary tension while you are delivering your word. This approach shows humility and demystifies the prophetic ministry.

- Be yourself! As you are delivering a prophetic word, do not submit to any form of intimidation that says you need to look or sound like someone else when you prophesy. God desires to use you just the way you are.

- In prophetic cultures that I develop in churches and ministries, I try to make it part of the culture to ask for feedback once you are done giving a prophetic word. I do this for two reasons. The first reason is that it gives people an "out" if they feel it is an incorrect prophetic word. We should never manipulate people into embracing our prophetic words because we feel insecure of being wrong. We need to honour people by giving them the opportunity to share their opinion of the word. Secondly, we ask for feedback because then if a part of our word is off, then we can fix it for next time. This way we can continually grow in our prophetic gift and delivery.

Cultivating A Prophetic Lifestyle

Prophetic Exercise

Now that you have learned how to receive, interpret, and deliver a prophetic word, we are going to activate what we have learned. In the last exercise, we were practicing hearing the voice of God for ourselves, whereas in this exercise we are going to practice hearing God for someone else.

We are going to do this in the form of asking God a question for someone. Remember that as you are waiting to hear a word from the Lord, to bounce what you hear off of the tips I gave you in this chapter concerning how to tell if the word you have received is from God.

Right now I want you to posture yourself to receive from God. Once you are in a posture to receive, ask the Lord to bring someone to mind who God wants to encourage through you.

Once God has brought someone to mind, ask Him this question:

"God, if this person were an animal, what type of animal would they be?"

Once God speaks to you, then ask Him this:

"How does this relate to their life, and how do

The Three Facets of Prophecy

you want to encourage them through this?"

As an example, God could have brought to mind an owl as you were listening, because this person walks in Godly wisdom.

Here is another question you could ask God:

"God if this person were a colour, what type of colour would they be? How does this relate to their life?"

Once you feel you have heard from the Lord, you can then discern how and when would be an appropriate way to share this word with the person who you felt God spoke to you about. Remember as you are delivering the word, to keep your prophetic delivery in accordance with the tips that I showed you concerning how to communicate a prophetic word properly.

Judging Prophetic Words

1 Thessalonians 5:19-21: "Do not quench the Spirit. Do not despise prophecies. Test all things; hold fast to what is good."

I want to take a moment to teach you how to judge whether a word is from the Lord or not when someone is giving you a prophetic word. Judging prophetic words is probably one of the most crucial lessons we need to learn as prophetic people if we are a part of a prophetic community. If we do not understand how to discern a "good word" from a "bad word", then a lot of damage can be done while prophesying or being recipients of someone else's word. I have met many people who have been wounded simply because they did not know how to discern the authenticity of what was being prophesied over them by someone else. This resulted in them feeling trapped in a word that was not from God.

As a prophetic leader, one of my job descriptions is to develop and oversee prophetic communities. I do a lot of training concerning how to prophesy, but in order to create healthy communities where the voice of the Lord is common, people need to be equipped in how to judge prophetic words properly. If I only teach people how to prophesy without teaching them how to judge words, then we would end up having dysfunctional cultures in churches concerning what is appropriate in the prophetic ministry.

1 Corinthians 14:29: "Let two or three prophets speak, and let the others judge."

Often when I would first arrive at a church to develop a prophetic culture, there would be people approaching me right, left and centre asking me to tell them whether the word they received from someone was from God or not. At first, since there has not yet been a culture established, the prophetic integrity of this church is fully dependent on me being there. However, after I have trained people to judge words,

Judging Prophetic Words

if someone gives a bad word to them, they know how to discern whether it is from the Lord or not. If it is not from God, then they know how to reject the word with honour. This way, we have prophetic communities that are self-sustaining, rather than a community that requires the leadership to constantly intervene in order to move forward in the prophetic.

We need to understand that as prophetic people, when someone gives us a word, it is essential that we judge the word before we apply it to our lives. Not only is it essential, but it is actually our responsibility. In the Old Testament, the full responsibility to discern the Lord's voice was dependent on he or she who spoke the word. The reason why the full weight of responsibility was on them, was because Holy Spirit did not abide in man in the Old Testament. Therefore, no one was able to discern what was God's word and what was not. Now, since we are all filled with the Spirit of God when we are born again, we carry the ability to discern, so therefore we are responsible for what we receive as truth. This is very important to understand while stewarding an internal revival. You are such a powerful person to the extent that you get to choose whether someone's external words affect your internal culture or not. You cannot always stop someone from saying something negative to you, but you are the one who decides whether it affects your inner being.

Cultivating A Prophetic Lifestyle

I am going to give you a list of ways to judge prophetic words properly.

- First off, does the word that you are receiving line up with the written Word of God? If it does not, then you have every right to disregard what is being said.

- Does the word build you up, encourage or comfort you? Remember, prophetic words should not condemn or judge. They call forth your potential (1 Corinthians 14:3).

- Does the word bear witness with your spirit? Holy Spirit abides in you, so if the word is from God then He will testify to the word's validity (1 Corinthians 2:10).

- Do you feel as though there are any manipulative motives behind the word? Every expression of an individual's spirit has to come through the filter of their soul. Sometimes when someone is wounded and has not had proper prophetic training, then they could be prophesying out of a place of hurt.

Judging Prophetic Words

An example would be, say, if someone said to you that God told them you are supposed to give them money. This would be a form of a manipulative word. God's word always honours free will. True love does not trap.

- If you receive more of a directional word from someone and you are unsure of its validity, bring the word to those who are in leadership above you to receive their input. If you are still unsure of its validity, then wait for God to confirm the word through other trusted sources.

- If the word that you are receiving from someone strikes any fear or discomfort in your heart, then run it by a leader who you trust. If we are going through a highly emotional season, sometimes our emotions will interpret something someone else says through a wounded lens. Therefore, a word intended to edify could come across as condemning. In these instances, it is good to get feedback from someone who is spiritually mature and who you trust. However, if this was in fact just a bad word, then you can disregard the word.

Disregarding Bad Words

If you feel as though someone is trying to give you a word and it does not edify, exhort or comfort you, then you have the right to disregard the word. Some people will let bad prophetic words influence them. However, we need to understand that we are so powerful that we can actually choose not to receive a word that does not build us up.

For the sake of practicality, I will give you a few tips in how you could turn down a bad prophetic word:

Say that someone you do not know comes up to you and says that they feel like God gave them a word for you. They say, "I feel like God is saying that you are about to come under a spiritual attack and that you have hidden pride which needs to be dealt with."

Now, obviously this is a really bad prophetic word, which is not from God. It does not build you up, encourage or comfort you. In fact, it is a word that condemns and strikes fear.

The person's heart posture will dictate how you can best respond to a word like this. If they are teachable, you can actually use this circumstance to help them grow in their prophetic delivery. You can say something like, "I appreciate you trying to give me a word, but I did not find it encouraging. Prophecy is actually intended to build people up." You can then

Judging Prophetic Words

begin to teach them how to properly deliver a word if it feels like an appropriate time to do so.

Some people give bad words because they simply do not know better, as the by-product of bad teaching, or no training at all. Others give bad words because they are purely trying to minister out of an insecurity, so therefore they will try to give condemning words to intimidate or to seem hyper-spiritual. If someone is giving you a bad word and they are doing it out of a bad heart, then you have every right to be more upfront about not receiving the word.

Being in ministry, I get a lot of people who take it upon themselves to try to correct things that they do not agree with in my ministry. Unfortunately, many people have the tendency to over-spiritualize their opinion and put the Lord's name on their accusations. If you are in the spotlight, it is essential to know how to not let people's bad prophetic words and opinions stick to you. I remember one time there was a man who read one of my books, and disagreed with a specific statement I made. This man contacted me saying that the Lord told him that He was going to curse my ministry and my finances because of the statement I made. I stopped the man and said, "Right now I put the cross between me and your words. I do not receive anything that you are saying because it is not the Lord." I immediately put up boundaries with my words to protect my heart, and then ended the conversation.

Could you imagine if I did not know how to disregard a bad word? I would have been in constant anxiety worrying that my ministry and finances would be cursed. This is why it is so important to know how to discern properly what is coming out of the mouths of others toward you, and how to not allow negative words to stick to you.

Some of you reading right now may have had negative "prophetic" words spoken over you in the past. Those words may have been given by someone with a good heart, yet their word was just not in line with what the Lord wants for your life. Or, the person may have spoken these things out of bitterness to intentionally to hurt you. Either way, God does not want you to carry these words that have brought you pain. If this is you, then here is a prayer that you can pray.

"Jesus, right now I repent for allowing these negative words to come into my heart. I wipe myself off from the lies of the enemy. I choose to not submit to the weight of these words any longer. Holy Spirit, shower me with truth about what the Father says about me. I am a child of God. My Father has grand plans for my life. I am protected by His love and by His truth. Thank you Lord that your words over me are filled with life, love, joy and peace."

The Four Revelatory Gifts

1 Corinthians 12:7-11: "The manifestation of the Spirit is given to each one for the profit of all: for to one is given the word of wisdom through the Spirit, to another the word of knowledge through the same Spirit, to another faith by the same Spirit, to another gifts of healings by the same Spirit, to another the working of miracles, to another prophecy, to another discerning of spirits, to another different kinds of tongues, to another the interpretation of tongues. But one and the same Spirit works all these things, distributing to each one individually as He wills."

Most people who have grown to a place of maturity in their prophetic gift will ebb and flow in the four revelatory gifts. In 1 Corinthians 12 there are four giftings that fall in line with the prophetic ministry. Those four gifts are: prophecy, words of knowledge, messages of wisdom and discerning of spirits.

We are going to walk through each gift to understand its function, and also how to move in each.

Prophecy

Since the majority of this book has been about the prophetic ministry, I will just briefly define the gift of prophecy. To give a message of prophecy is to call forth who God has created someone to be. Prophetic words can be messages from the Father's heart, messages about someone's calling, revelation concerning an individual's future, etc.

Word of Knowledge

While prophecy is often speaking about the future, or what the Father is speaking into the present, words of knowledge pertain to what has already occurred in the past or what is taking place in the present.

The Four Revelatory Gifts

Jesus often utilized words of knowledge throughout His ministry:

John 1:47-49: "Jesus saw Nathanael coming toward Him, and said of him, 'Behold, an Israelite indeed, in whom is no deceit!' Nathanael said to Him, 'How do You know me?' Jesus answered and said to him, 'Before Philip called you, when you were under the fig tree, I saw you.' Nathanael answered and said to Him, 'Rabbi, You are the Son of God! You are the King of Israel!'"

John 4:16-18: "Jesus said to her, 'Go, call your husband, and come here.' The woman answered and said, 'I have no husband.' Jesus said to her, 'You have well said, 'I have no husband,' 'for you have had five husbands, and the one whom you now have is not your husband; in that you spoke truly.'"

Moses moved powerfully in a gift of knowledge. Most theologians believe that Moses was the author of the book of Genesis. If this is true, then Moses must have received amazing insight through divine revelation concerning events that took place before he was even born. I am sure that there must have been some form of documented history concerning some of the things that were recorded in Genesis. However, I cannot see how Moses would have documented something such as the creation account in such detail without experiencing it himself. He probably experienced these things through visions and dreams.

Prophetic words and words of knowledge are two of my most common and effective tools for evangelism. A while back, I took a young friend of mine who was only 15 years old at the time down to a specific store with me. We were hanging out, when Holy Spirit began to move. We walked past two women in the make-up aisle when I suddenly felt a gentle pain in my left ankle. I do not usually get pain in my ankle, so I knew that this was a word of knowledge for one of these women.

We walked up to the women and introduced ourselves. I then said to the younger woman, "This might be a weird question, but do you have any pain in your body at all?"

The woman responded, saying that she had no pain in her body. Since I stepped out in faith, the Lord honoured my obedience by giving me more details for the word of knowledge. I replied, saying, "Are you sure you didn't hurt your left ankle while dancing two weeks ago?"

Her jaw dropped. She told me that two weeks ago while dancing she slipped and hurt her ankle.

The Four Revelatory Gifts

I motioned to my young friend and said to her, "If you let my friend here pray for you, then God is going to heal your ankle."

My friend got down and laid his hands on her ankle and she was completely healed.

Since there was a grace for words of knowledge, we kept ministering to people. We walked by an older woman and I instantly felt a pain in my chest. I also felt pain in my joints and the words "terminally ill" came into my head. I walked up to her and her family. I said to the woman, "I am a Christian and I felt like God told me that He wants to heal any pain that you get in your joints, and of a terminal illness having to do with your chest. Does this make sense to you?"

The woman nodded her head and immediately walked away in tears. I asked her son and daughter who were with her why she walked away. They began to tell me that their mother had an appointment with her doctor one week ago and was told that she had cancer in her chest.

I looked down the aisle that the woman had walked down and saw her huddled over weeping. When I called her over to me, she wept and embraced me in a hug. I prayed over her and all of the pain left her joints and chest. She felt the presence of God and a peace that she said she had never experienced in her whole life.

Cultivating A Prophetic Lifestyle

My friend and I walked around the store for about 40 minutes and saw two people's ankles healed and one woman who I believe was healed of cancer, whose joints were also healed. We saw three people's backs healed, one person's broken heel healed and a man's right foot healed. We also saw a man who had some form of kidney disease healed and a woman's hips realigned. This place was in full blown revival because we decided to listen to what Holy Spirit was saying to us through words of knowledge.

Receiving a word of knowledge for healing can be as easy as feeling a subtle pain in your body that you have not felt before, or feeling God highlighting a body part to you. Often we dismiss the Lord speaking in this way because we assume He should speak in more of a supernatural way; however, this is a way that He will often give words of knowledge. Test this out the next time you go to the grocery store, or to the mall. Ask Holy Spirit to give you a word of knowledge, and then be extra sensitive to what you feel in your body when you are in the store and while around people.

I believe that Jesus walked in something greater than a word of knowledge gifting. I believe that Jesus operated under the ministry of the Spirit of knowledge (Isaiah 11:2). The difference is that, while ministering in words of knowledge, we receive a small amount of knowledge concerning who someone is. However, when we minister under the Spirit of knowledge, we

The Four Revelatory Gifts

can have a more complete understanding of someone.

Remember John 2:24-25: "Jesus did not commit Himself to them, because He knew all men, and had no need that anyone should testify of man, for He knew what was in man." Jesus actually had a fuller understanding of every man and woman. Numerous times throughout the gospel there is even record of Jesus knowing people's thoughts (Matthew 9:4, Matthew 12:25, Luke 5:22, Luke 6:8, Luke 11:17).

When I was younger, the Lord brought me through an interesting season where He was training me in how to grow my knowledge of people. I would to go to a restaurant with a group of friends (usually around 12 people or so), and I would go from person to person asking Holy Spirit questions about them. I would look at the first person and ask Holy Spirit what spiritual gifts they excelled in most and about the calling over their lives. Then I would do this with the second person. I would ask for all 12 people. I would then start again at the first person and ask Holy Spirit what season in life they had most recently come out of, what season they were presently in, and what their next season in life would look like. I would again go through all 12 people. By the end I would have a good idea of who every person at that table was.

Now, since I have developed my ears to listen in this way, when I look at someone I will have a decent understanding of who that person is. I obviously do not know everything, because we all see and know in part. However, I have found this level of discernment tremendously beneficial while being in ministry. In fact, it would be highly beneficial for anyone in any form of leadership. It makes apostolic building much simpler when you can prophetically read people's gifts and callings. Fathering and mothering people is more effective when we understand people's past, present and future seasons. Moving in this level of knowledge concerning people can help us to walk alongside of them in a profound capacity because we are then able to see them the way God sees them.

Message of Wisdom

I believe there is about to be a drastic increase of understanding concerning messages of wisdom throughout the global church. A message of wisdom is a word from the Lord which unlocks situations.

For example, if you were wanting to build a house, you could say that prophecy would show you what the future house in completion looks like. Knowledge would show you how to use the tools to get the job done, and wisdom would show you what order to do things to finish as quick and efficiently as possible.

The Four Revelatory Gifts

Moses walked in a weighty message of wisdom gift. Exodus 18:13 says that Moses would sit from morning until evening giving wisdom to every Israelite who needed counsel.

One time, while in a worship service, I was worshipping in the back of the church when I suddenly had an angelic experience that launched me into profound influence in my ministry as a prophetic leader. In the church, I saw an angel standing in front of me wearing fine linen. I was unaware if anyone else could see what I was seeing or not. All of a sudden, the angel materialized a small silver key with a blue gem stone on it from its pocket. The angel then went on to hand me the key.

I asked Holy Spirit what the key that was handed to me represented. He said, "This key is the message of wisdom I have called you to carry. With messages of wisdom, you can unlock entire groups of people and churches into their destinies. You can guide the influential so that they will not stray from My will."

Ever since this encounter, I have been contacted by those who have great influence from different streams of society who need prophetic guidance. I work with many leaders in this capacity, many of whom are pastors and apostolic leaders in the church. I have also prophetically advised government leaders, significant business leaders and well known people in the film and music industry. When pastors and apostles seek me out, they will often ask me to consult with the Lord concerning reoccurring problems which they do not know how to fix. I will then wait on the Lord to discern the church's or ministry's road block and how they can remove it to walk in all that God has for them.

I will share a story with you: A while ago, a pastor of a church of about 60 people called me. The pastor explained that his entire church had fallen into a state where no sign of spiritual growth had occurred for years.

I sat in on one of their services and as I waited on the Lord, I observed what was taking place in the atmosphere. As the pastor would teach, I saw in the spirit a wall standing in front of him. Before his words could penetrate the hearts of the congregation members, his words would hit the wall and fall to the ground.

Holy Spirit showed me that there was something within the history of the church that needed to be healed. He revealed to me that in the 1980's there was a situation with the leadership of that church which was not dealt with in an honouring way. Ever since this point, there has been a lack of trust from the congregation toward the pastoral leaders of the church. Holy Spirit then told me that if the leadership would do a public repentance on behalf of the past leaders, that the wall of offense would be broken down.

The Four Revelatory Gifts

I shared with the pastor what I had discerned. Once the pastor brought the word to the eldership, they prayed and decided to move ahead with a service of repentance and reconciliation. Right after the reconciliation service took place, the youth pastor was praying in his office when he audibly heard a wall crack and fall. After this service, there was so much trust rebuilt between the congregation and leadership team that for the next three weeks, the offering more than tripled in number.

We can see how messages of wisdom can unlock situations that we may find ourselves in. I have noticed that many highly pastoral people walk in high levels of message of wisdom gifts without even realizing it. When a pastoral person is ministering to someone, they might find themselves giving Holy Spirit led advice to bring alignment to people's lives or relationships. A lot of the time, this is them actually relaying what Holy Spirit is giving them to say to the person to bring restoration in their lives.

Messages of wisdom will at times come across as Spirit led direction. Now, in saying that I need to set up the proper boundaries around that statement. I would not recommend to make a habit of giving directional prophetic words if you are not seasoned in the prophetic ministry. When I say "seasoned in the prophetic", I do not mean that you have given a few prophetic words here or there. I mean that you have allowed God to tune your ears to hear His voice, and therefore are trusted by people of Godly character and integrity in your ability to hear the Lord. Even for those who are seasoned in the prophetic ministry, we need to take a posture of humility while delivering such words. Vocabulary such as, "I feel that the Lord is saying..." is always a great approach, instead of saying, "This is what God said for you to do."

Warning words from God can be another form of message of wisdom. A word of warning is different from a word of judgement. Much like correctional words, I believe that words of warning are carried out best in the context of relationship. I am not saying that the Lord would not do otherwise, however, I have seen these words function the healthiest in relationships. If a word of warning is being given, it should be delivered with much integrity and prayer.

Discerning of Spirits

I believe that the gift of discerning of spirits is one of the most misunderstood gifts recorded in 1 Corinthians 12. People have often limited this gift to only discerning demonic spirits. One of the purposes for discerning of spirits is to discern demonic spirits that are tormenting people; however, this is probably only 20% of the gift's function. This gift is not called

The Four Revelatory Gifts

"discerning of demonic spirits", rather, it is more general than specific. This gift is also for discerning angelic spirits, human spirits and most importantly, to discern what Holy Spirit is doing.

While prophecy is a more internalized gift, as in we hear Holy Spirit speaking from within, discerning of spirits is externally tapping into what is happening in the atmosphere around us. Sometimes discerning of spirits will often work the same way as words of knowledge. A discerning person could sit next to someone who is depressed and they will begin to feel symptoms of depression themselves even if they have never felt that way before.

When I first began moving in discerning of spirits, I would walk into a place like a coffee shop, and would at times feel overwhelmed because I could externally feel what everyone was going through. As a discerning person, I had to learn to distinguish other people's dysfunctions from my reality. Very discerning people need to learn how to not take ownership for what is not theirs. To give you an example: If you walk into a room and a suicidal thought pops into your head when you have never had a suicidal thought before, you more than likely do not have to go for inner healing or deliverance. You could very well be tapping into the fact that there is someone in the room who struggles with having thoughts of suicide.

Cultivating A Prophetic Lifestyle

Discerning of spirits has two steps to it. First, we discern what is occurring externally. Second, we discern internally what Holy Spirit is saying about it. Discerning what Holy Spirit is saying is crucial. I know many who move in this type of gifting who feel burdened when they discern something. They feel as though they have spiritual insight and information, yet do not know the practical application. Logically trying to figure out how to deal with what you discern could get you in a lot of trouble. It could even lead you down a path of believing that everything you discern is your responsibility to deal with. If that were the case, spiritually discerning people would burn out very quickly. Sometimes we discern things because Holy Spirit wants to give insight into how we can bring change. Other times, we discern things simply because we are discerning. Our responsibility is to be in communication with Holy Spirit and to keep in step with what He is doing and saying.

Sometimes discerning people will struggle with prophetic delivery. The struggle comes because discerning people will often see what is occurring in the spirit realm, where angels and demons battle. Discerning people will often discern specific demonic spirits that are tormenting individuals, so therefore they may try and give their word in an incorrect context. I am sure some of you have experienced words being spoken such as, "You have a spirit of confusion over you and God wants to deliver you of it." Even if the person truly did discern this, I believe that this is an improper way to share what is being discerned.

If I discern that someone has a spirit of confusion tormenting them and just tell them this, I am actually pointing them to the demonic activity in their lives, therefore could be empowering it. I could be empowering it by striking fear in their heart.

When we discern something demonic in the spirit realm, then we can do what I call "flipping a word". Instead of pointing people to their problem, we can instead prophesy from the standpoint of victory. We are seated in heavenly places in Christ (Ephesians 2:6), so therefore we can see from the perspective of how the Father sees things.

For example, if you were to discern that someone was inflicted with a spirit of confusion, then you could simply declare the opposite. You could declare what God is desiring to establish in their life. You could say something like, "God is bringing you into a season of clarity, where things that haven't made much sense will now be clear." See, you do not even have to mention the spirit of confusion, because when you speak truth, the truth dethrones the lie. The light casts out the darkness. If you meet someone who struggles with fits of anger, you do not have to tell them that there is a spirit of anger over them. Just tell them what the Father sees. You could say something like, "God is releasing joy over you." As discerning people, if we can begin to learn how to flip

Cultivating A Prophetic Lifestyle

our words, then we will see a lot less people hurt by our words, and a lot more people set free from their torment.

As I have mentioned, this gift has far more to it than simply discerning demonic spirits. With discerning of spirits, we can also discern angels, human spirits and Holy Spirit. For the sake of clarity, I will give you an example of what it could look like if you were discerning a human spirit.

Many years ago, I was eating in the food court of a mall, when suddenly, I felt the atmosphere shift. I thought to myself, "It feels like the international prophet who commissioned me into ministry is in the mall." I did not even know if this particular man was in the city. However, I walked around the food court to see if he was there, and found him walking around the mall. I walked over to him, and was able to have a conversation with one of my role models of the faith.

Through discerning of spirits, I was actually able to discern that this man was in the vicinity of me, even though I did not even know if he was in the same nation at the time. Discerning human spirits can come in handy as you are growing in delivering prophetic words. It is in our spirit where our calling, mantles, anointings and giftings abide. If you are paying attention with your discernment, you will be able to notice that when you are around someone who is primarily gifted in business, because of what they

The Four Revelatory Gifts

carry in their spirit, it feels very different in contrast to if you were around someone whose primary ministry is intercession and prayer. This form of discerning spirits can actually help you to narrow in on your prophetic words to speak directly to someone's calling.

I believe that many worship leaders who flow prophetically during worship carry an incredible gift of discerning of spirits. They might not be discerning demonic spirits, however, as worship leaders, their job is to discern the spiritual climate of the meeting, and then flow musically in a way that will partner with what Holy Spirit wants to accomplish in the room.

Jesus was absolutely brilliant in how He discerned the spirit realm. Read Mark 5:25-31: "Now a certain woman had a flow of blood for twelve years, and had suffered many things from many physicians. She had spent all that she had and was no better, but rather grew worse. When she heard about Jesus, she came behind Him in the crowd and touched His garment. For she said, 'If only I may touch His clothes, I shall be made well.' Immediately the fountain of her blood was dried up, and she felt in her body that she was healed of the affliction. And Jesus, immediately knowing in Himself that power had gone out of Him, turned around in the crowd and said, 'Who touched My clothes?' But His disciples said to Him, 'You see the multitude thronging You, and You say, 'Who touched Me?'"

Cultivating A Prophetic Lifestyle

In this scenario Jesus is in a mob of people, shoulder to shoulder. One woman touches the hem of His garment and He feels power go out from Him. Jesus was so tuned in to what was happening in the spirit realm, that He noticed when a woman took a piece of the kingdom off of Him by faith. His spiritual senses were so developed, that even though He was crammed in a group of people, He noticed the slightest shift in the spirit realm.

We carry the kingdom everywhere we go. Whether you know it or not, when you walk into a room, the atmosphere shifts and changes because of who you are. Sometimes I wonder how much is being accomplished for the kingdom when we just show up somewhere. I can guarantee that people experience freedom from their depression and anxieties simply because we get around them and carry a perfect culture of peace and joy. Breakthrough and healing from sickness and pain occurs, because the kingdom of heaven dwells inside of us (Luke 17:21). We can actually develop our discernment to the point where when we walk into a room, we are able to tell who is being influenced by the joy and peace of heaven that we carry. We can actually come to a place where our spiritual senses are so developed that we are completely aware of what Holy Spirit is doing in our surroundings, just as Jesus was.

Chapter Summary

While reading this chapter, I am sure that you have noticed that out of the four revelatory gifts, you may be more gifted in some gifts than others. For those of you who are more evangelistic, you may have more of a natural gifting in words of knowledge, whereas those of you who are more pastoral may have more of a pull to messages of wisdom or discernment. While we will always have spiritual gifts that we function in more primarily, I believe that it is quite possible for us to walk in all of the gifts of the Spirit to some degree. Jesus is our prime example in how to live a kingdom lifestyle, and He walked in all of the gifts of the Spirit. God's heart is to add tools to your tool belt, so that you can effectively demonstrate His love to people and advance His kingdom wherever you go.

Prophetic Exercise

In the previous prophetic exercises, I had you ask God a specific question concerning someone to help you discern the voice of the Lord. In this exercise, we are going to ask God a much more general question.

Cultivating A Prophetic Lifestyle

Once you have postured yourself to receive from the Lord, ask Him to bring someone to mind who He wants to encourage through you.

Once He has brought someone to mind, ask Him this question:

"God, what is it that you want to say to this person?"

Still your mind and allow God to show you what He wants to show you. He may speak to you about their calling. He may give you a timely word for the season of life they are in. He may give you a word of knowledge. Whatever you feel He shows you, test the prophetic word, and allow the Lord to help you discern what a proper way would be for you to deliver this word.

Something to always remember about moving in the prophetic ministry, is that you will grow in your gifting by walking in friendship with the Lord and by utilizing it. For those of you who have been activated in hearing God's voice thus far, then I would encourage you to keep at it. God wants to use you as His prophetic mouthpiece on the earth. You were created to be a vessel for Him to speak through to His children throughout the earth.

Common Pitfalls of the Prophetic Ministry

Since I have much experience training people in the prophetic ministry, I have become quite familiar with understanding the pitfalls that can follow highly prophetic people and prophets. Often highly prophetic people slip into many of these mindsets without even realizing that they are doing it. Throughout this chapter, I want to journey with you through some of the different pitfalls of the prophetic ministry.

Gnosticism

In the last decade or so, there has been a vast amount of revelation hitting the church concerning prophetic experiences. God has been revealing to the church the accessibility and invitation that we have to different experiences and encounters that men and women of God have had in Biblical times. These are things that we have an access to through the cross.

Some of these encounters that God has been shining light on involve: angelic visitations (Matthew 4:11), being transported (Acts 8:26-40), out-of-body experiences (2 Kings 5:26), and third-heaven encounters (Isaiah 6, Ezekiel 1, Daniel 7). Other types of encounters involve visitations from saints who have already passed on to be with the Lord (Matthew 17), and visitations from the Lord Himself (Acts 9:1-19).

Prophetic encounters are along the mystical side of prophecy. Many try to steer away from this realm of Christianity, even though prophetic encounters with God can be a pivotal tool to wholeness and Christlikeness. I encourage any prophet or prophetic leader who develops prophetic communities to create space for prophetic experiences. I myself have trained many in how to position themselves to experience prophetic encounters.

Common Pitfalls of the Prophetic Ministry

Some elements of prophetic encounters can come across as weird. However, I believe that a more appropriate way to describe it would be to say that it is supernatural. Supernatural things have a tendency to offend our minds because the supernatural stretches beyond the laws of the natural. As intellectuals, we can have a tendency to dismiss whatever does not fit into our intellectual grid. However, we need to learn to be a people who do not fix our eyes on what is seen, but rather on what is unseen (2 Corinthians 4:18).

Often when God restores revelation to the church, there are those who take these new truths to unhealthy extremes. This is where we can step into some pitfalls with prophetic encounters. I am an advocate for prophetic experiences, however, such things need to be sourced by love, and stewarded with integrity. I know many highly prophetic people where such experiences are very common because there is a grace for them to experience the mystical. If there is a grace to see and hear the word of the Lord in a more mystical way, yet we are not rooted in love and grounded in Godly character, there can often be a pull towards forms of gnosticism.

Gnosticism was a belief back in Biblical times that taught against Jesus' divinity, and pushed people into the worship of man's spirit. Gnosticism leads people in the direction of dismissing the importance of anything of the natural realm, only seeing value with things that are potently spiritual or mystical.

I have met many who have diligently pursued prophetic encounters, yet were not rooted in relationship with the Lord. What this did was it caused them to transition from a place of deeming prophetic encounters as a tool to know the Lord more, into believing that an encounter was the end goal. If our goal in desiring prophetic encounters is not to know the Lord more in friendship, then we are likely doing it out of an unhealthy curiosity for the supernatural, or out of an insecurity to be deemed as spiritual. Pursuing such experiences with a poor heart posture can open up many doors for deception, such as a worship of spiritual experiences, gnosticism and even the occult.

Not only should we be rooted in hunger to know the Lord more if we are seeking such experiences, but we should also be rooted in the written Word of God, the Bible. Every day I am blown away by the depth of scripture. It is such an amazing tool that God has given us to understand His heart and character. When pursuing prophetic encounters, the Bible is what will keep us rooted in truth. I have seen many people go off the deep end in what they perceive is truth, because they see more validity in what they have felt prophetically compared to what is written in scripture. As a result, their doctrine is 90% rooted in encounter, and 10% rooted in the Bible. We always need to remember that the prophetic word will always submit to the written word of God. Everything we experience prophetically may not be written in black and white in the Bible, but scripture should always support what you experience. The prophetic should never contradict scripture because God's Word is not divided.

Prophetic encounters are a tool to encounter the love of God. What they should do is infuse you with love so that you can love those around you better. In the scriptural accounts of prophetic encounters throughout the Bible, there was a natural manifestation from such experiences. This means that you could test the validity of the encounter, by its fruit. Ezekiel's heavenly encounter in Ezekiel 1 resulted in him stepping into his prophetic calling to bring change to Israel. Paul the apostle's encounter when Jesus came to him in Acts 9, launched him into understanding the heart of God for himself, so that he could be an apostle to the nations. It is fine to hunger for supernatural encounters, however, we need to do it from a place of hunger to encounter the love of God. This should result in us loving those around us better. If someone is having these types of encounters, yet they are not expressing more love as the byproduct, then I believe that we have the right to question the legitimacy of the encounter.

Dismissing the Practical

Highly prophetic people will often have the tendency to naturally excel in things that are spiritual. Since there is such a grace to tap into things of the spirit, there can often be a lack of understanding of the importance of things that are more practical. This will often result in people being tremendously gifted, yet having very noticeable holes in their life skills.

Before I was in full time ministry, I thought that in order to have a legitimate ministry, all that I would need to do is know how to teach well, know how to prophesy accurately and have enough faith to see the sick healed. When I did start up my ministry, I was blown away by how practical you need to think to run something such as a ministry with excellence. I quickly began to understand that even if I can move in the gifts of the Spirit, if I do not have a focus on administration, then I will not be able to impact as many people as I would like to with these gifts.

There is a side to moving in the Spirit which is completely supernatural, yet there is another side that is tremendously practical as well. I need to know how to prophesy, as well as know how to keep on top of bookings for speaking engagements. I need to know how to pray for the sick, as well as how to have good people skills to properly interact with other leaders throughout the world. If I were not willing to

Common Pitfalls of the Prophetic Ministry

continually grow in my faith for the supernatural as well as my life skills in my ministry, it would give the enemy a huge foot in to affect the impact that I now get to make for the advancement of the kingdom of heaven. In fact, I have met many people who have a great call to minister to the masses, whether that is in the church or in the marketplace. These are people who have been greatly gifted by God. Yet, because of a lack of a willingness to grow in practical life skills their level of influence is drastically minimized.

It is not false humility to acknowledge your weaknesses or areas that you need to grow in. As for myself, I have found tremendous value in acknowledging that one of my weaknesses as an individual is practicality. This is not everyone's weakness. However, I know that it is not something that I naturally excel in. In recognizing this with myself, I have had the opportunity to surround myself with many people who could coach me in more practical ways, such as my finances, my health and my relationships. I also surround myself with different business leaders to help give counsel and insight as to how I should run the practical side of my ministry. Just because practicality is not an area that I naturally thrive in, this cannot be used as an excuse for me to not allow God to develop my practical life skills.

Whether it is through our health, finances, relationships, or any other aspect of life, we need to see how the supernatural and the practical are supposed to blend together in us. I would go as far as to say that in order to walk in maturity as a spiritual person, we need to be a place where both the supernatural and the practical marry.

The Tyranny of Assumption

Something I have often observed while working with different prophetic groups, is that many will have the tendency to slip into the tyranny of assumption. What I mean by this, is that those who are highly prophetic can have a habit of trusting their discernment more than they trust those who they are in covenant relationships with. I will paint a picture for you:

Say that you are in close relationship with someone. We will call her Betty. You have known Betty for a few years now and have spent much time with her. One day at church, you see Betty and as you are crossing paths, it almost seems as though she is trying to avoid eye contact with you. This is highly unlike Betty, considering that usually she is a Chatty Kathy. You are now finding yourself confused by her actions. Soon you find yourself frantically searching through your memory, trying to see if you can think of what you may have done to offend her. You then feel your confusion concerning the situation evolving to

Common Pitfalls of the Prophetic Ministry

frustration towards her. This leads your mind to begin to assume what Betty is feeling toward you, which can lead us down a scary road when assumption is in control of the wheel.

In a prophetic community where there is a lack of training on kingdom relationships, this can go south very quickly. Someone who does not know how to wield their discernment gift yet with maturity, may begin to assume things about the person who they are in conflict with, which are in fact not true. In their hurt, based on what they are assuming, they then can easily label that assumption as "discernment". All of a sudden there is a clear wedge within a relationship simply due to a lack of understanding concerning healthy communication.

For those who have revelation concerning how to do healthy conflict, the obvious solution would have been to approach Betty, asking her if something is wrong, for the sake of not allowing assumption to swell. However, for those who may be highly gifted prophetically, there could be a tendency to have more trust in gifting, compared to talking things through in relationships.

Often when we are in an emotional situation, such as in relationships, our emotions can cloud our discernment. If you are only depending on your discernment in a situation such as this, then in the name of "discernment" we can then easily begin to build a case toward someone. We could be creating unnecessary distance with them, simply because we are not willing to do healthy communication. This could then even result in us talking badly about this person to others, which begins stepping into the territory of gossip.

It is of utmost importance that those who are primarily geared towards gifts of discernment, receive proper pastoral training in how to walk in relationships in a healthy manner. If a discerning person struggles with insecurity, they could think that they are discerning other people's offenses toward them. This will often create a void of assumption for the enemy to speak lies. Discerning people need to learn how to do healthy conflict and communication to disarm offense that may be made up. Probably some of the best advice I can give an emerging leader is this: revival is messy. Walking in relationships with people is messy. Instead of assuming other's faults and complaining about the mess, we need to learn how to grab a mop and clean it up. We need to learn how to do healthy conflict and communication well in our relationships if we ever want to be part of a team. Instead of only depending on our gifts, we need to allow God to develop our people skills in our relationships. Discernment and assumption are two different things entirely, so we cannot merge them. Discernment is when God gives you insight into a situation, whereas assumption is making an intellectual or emotional analysis, which could easily be tainted by whatever is occurring within the realm of the soul.

Rejection and Isolation

One of the most common pitfalls for highly prophetic people and prophets is isolation. The reason being, that many highly prophetic people hear from the Lord in a way that seems uncommon. If they are in circles where the things of the Spirit are not embraced, then this could bring on much rejection due to people's lack of understanding concerning the prophetic ministry. I have met many highly prophetic people who have experienced heart breaking rejection from the church. I myself have gone through much rejection from the church, due to the call that is over my life and the uniqueness of my relationship with the Lord. That being said, in order for a prophetic person to cultivate a healthy prophetic lifestyle, they need to be woven into relationship within the family of God. One of the quickest ways to fall into deception as a prophetic person is by stepping out of community.

Time and time again I have met prophetic people who because of wounding, try to avoid being accountable in relationships. Often prophetic people will interpret the freedom that the cross granted us as freedom from commitment. They can slip into a lie which assumes that their gift works better apart from covering and accountability because it feels more free. If you are reading this and you fall into this category, I will tell you first hand: trying to operate as a prophetic person apart from community and accountability will lead you down a long road of wounding. The only way you will be able to reach your full potential as a prophetic person, is by being around others who can build into your weak areas. By yourself you will have clear blind spots, whereas in community those with different personalities and giftings will begin to form Jesus in the areas where you lack. That being said, while there may be people around us who we face rejection from, every one of us should also be surrounding ourselves with those who receive us as we are, who we can walk in covenant relationships with. Loneliness is not holiness, it is bondage. You were not created to be alone. You were created to know that you belong.

If we choose to be separate from the body of Christ due to fears of rejection, we are robbing the prophetic ministry from the church. We need to find healthy accountability instead of attempting to adopt principles and a heart posture of individualism.

The church needs the prophetic ministry. The prophetic ministry reconciles the church as a family by revealing the body's diversity in all of its callings, mantels, anointings, giftings, skills and talents. Prophecy shows the church that it cannot function properly when it is divided, and that every aspect of

Common Pitfalls of the Prophetic Ministry

God through His children has precious value.

If you are reading this and you have felt rejection from the church because of your prophetic gift, as a leader in the church, and on behalf of the church, I apologize to you. I declare over you that you are irreplaceable in the heart of God, and valuable in the kingdom of heaven. There is a place in the family of God that fits who you are perfectly. You were not created to walk alone. You were created to know that you belong. I pray that Jesus surrounds you with those who will both accept and love you. I pray that fathers and mothers of the faith will come around you to help you steward and nurture the calling over your life.

Manipulation and Control

Manipulation and control can be some of the more dangerous and extreme pitfalls for the prophetic ministry. The reason why is that these two pitfalls do not only hurt the person operating in them, but they could end up wounding many people. When prophetic people have slipped into a deep wound of rejection from the church, it can be tempting for them to believe that the entire church is in rebellion towards God. This can spark significant spiritual pride in an individual, considering that they are believing that the whole church is in the wrong, and they themselves are in the right. While it is true that none of us has a full revelation of who God is, it is a very presumptuous assumption to assume that we have the right to blatantly and bluntly call out what we consider rebellion in those who God has appointed. We should be leaving such judgements to God. While it takes deep heart wounding to assume that the entire church is in rebellion, I have seen the enemy use this level of hurt to take a few individuals down a road of much greater deception. Out of a place of hurt and pride, these people would try to operate in prophetic giftings toward the church from a place of tremendous wounding and bitterness. This would result in them manipulating and controlling others with their prophetic gift.

Matthew 7:15-16: "Beware of false prophets, who come to you in sheep's clothing, but inwardly they are ravenous wolves. You will know them by their fruits."

The difference between true prophets as opposed to false prophets, is that true prophets point to Jesus, whereas false prophets point to themselves. When I use the term "false prophet", I am not referring to someone who has given an incorrect prophetic word, because we are all learning and growing in how we

Common Pitfalls of the Prophetic Ministry

hear the Lord. I am referring to those who, out of pride, use their prophetic gifting to intentionally manipulate and control others because they are wounded. I honestly do not use the term "false prophet" often, and when I do, I am very careful in doing so. In fact, I have met very few people who I believe have walked in this level of deception. However, we need to be aware of the schemes of the enemy through false prophets. We also need to be testing our own hearts to make sure that we are ministering from a place of love, instead of from soulish desires.

False prophets minister out of a place of wounding and insecurity. Since they are hurt, they will often use their gift as means for attention and to manipulate. Something I have seen is a common characteristic of false prophets, is that they have a tendency to come into churches, and use their gift as a way to trick vulnerable church members into believing that the leadership is in rebellion. The false prophet will then try to take a place of leadership over those whom they have deceived. This of course brings division within churches. False prophets operate in high levels of manipulation, and have a reputation for twisting scripture to lure people into their self-promoting theologies and doctrines.

Those who walk in this level of deception have often been hurt by the church, so therefore walk in a lone ranger mentality. Someone who is walking in

Cultivating A Prophetic Lifestyle

maturity in the office of a prophet will not do so independently from the church, just as prophets in the Old Testament did not function as prophets apart from Israel. That being said, if you are not recognized as a prophet in a church, it does not matter how gifted you feel you are. You have no right to try and operate in authority that has not been released to you by leadership. Prophets are supposed to function alongside of those in authority, not against those in authority. Even if you are a well-known prophet throughout the nations, when you come into a local house to minister, you need to submit to the local authorities.

Pastors, beware of false prophets. If one tries to operate in your church, do not be intimidated by them. Do not be swayed by impressive gifting if their character does not add up. If they are turning people away from Christ and attempting to dethrone you as a leader, then do what is necessary to protect those who God has entrusted to you.

False prophets will often live their lives from a Messiah complex, tricking people into believing that they are the only ones who carry the authority to bring freedom to others. Matthew 7:16 says, "You will know them by their fruit." A false prophet's fruit will be a trail of broken people who are dependent on them, whereas a true prophet's fruit will be sons and daughters who build up the church through the prophetic ministry.

Common Pitfalls of the Prophetic Ministry

God has called His true prophets and prophetesses to be fathers and mothers in the church. Many prophets in the Old Testament have the reputation of being borderline militant. Moses stands in contrast to many of the other prophets in the Old Testament. Moses was not just a prophet to Israel, he was also a father and pastor to Israel. Deuteronomy 9 tells of when Moses was on Mount Sinai receiving the commandments of God. God then spoke to Moses, telling Him that the Israelites had rebelled against Him. God spoke to Moses in Deuteronomy 9:14 and said, "Let Me alone, that I may destroy them and blot out their name from under heaven; and I will make of you a nation mightier and greater than they."

Out of a desire to have a great name, Moses could have taken this offer to be a great nation. However, since he loved the Israelites, he laid facedown for 40 days and 40 nights fasting and interceding for Israel that God would reconsider (Deuteronomy 9:18). The mark of a mature prophet is the ability to lay down their life for God's children, out of love.

Ephesians 2:19-20: "Now, therefore, you are no longer strangers and foreigners, but fellow citizens with the saints and members of the household of God, having been built on the foundation of the apostles and prophets, Jesus Christ Himself being the chief cornerstone."

To be a prophet is not to lord over people. It is not to manipulate or control out of pride. It is to become the greatest servant. It is not a ministry where you stand above everyone; it is foundational. You take the posture of a servant to all, believing that everyone you serve by training will reach higher heights than you yourself do.

Friendship with God

Jeremiah 9:23-24: "Thus says the Lord: 'Let not the wise man glory in his wisdom, let not the mighty man glory in his might, nor let the rich man glory in his riches; But let him who glories glory in this, that he understands and knows Me...'"

What you are about to read in this chapter is the greatest key that I can give concerning the prophetic ministry. I am convinced that the greatest thing that you can ever invest your time into, is growing deeper in knowing the Lord in friendship. God is the most consistent person I have ever known. He is the same yesterday, today and forever. Even though God is consistent in who He is, since His love is so grand, I have never experienced two days that are the same since meeting Him. Every day is a new adventure. When you are truly following Jesus, predictability ceases to exist because in His company no one truly knows where they are going. Every moment with Him is an invitation to explore the unknown. It is an open door giving you the opportunity to experience true adventure.

When I had first met the Lord when I was 16 years old, I dedicated my life to knowing Him. Every day after school or work I would come home, drop off my bag, and head outside to walk with Jesus for four to six hours. When I would wake up on my days off, I often wouldn't even turn on my light. I would just lay praying and spending time with God for eight to 12 hours, before I even got out of bed. In this period of my life, there were times when I would save up my money so I could take time off of work for four months at a time. On my time off, I would soak with Jesus in His presence for about 14 hours per day. My first four years of knowing the Lord consisted of extended times and seasons in His presence in this way.

In these extended times with the Lord, I remember people commenting to me about the discipline that I had walked in, to be able to pray for such long periods of time. Looking back now, I know that my ability to spend this much time in prayer had absolutely nothing to do with discipline. It had everything to do with infatuation. I had allowed myself to become infatuated with Jesus. It was in this place where my ears began to be refined to hear His voice. It was in this place where my heart was softened to understand the feelings of His heart. Obviously, not all of us have this much free time to spend hours upon hours, one on one with the Lord. For me this was a very set apart and God ordained time. I believe that coming to this place of infatuation with the Lord has less to do with time spent, than it has to do with a heart to know Him. Intimacy brings a greater depth to anointing than gifting does. In fact, I believe that the most fruitful ministry does not come from impressive credentials, but from being in the secret place with God.

Something that I have learned while working with many prophetic leaders and by developing multiple prophetic communities, is that there is a very big difference between someone who prophesies from gifting, compared to friendship. Take a look at this with me:

Balaam from Numbers 22 had a weighty prophetic gift. He could give accurate prophetic words and predict the future. Balaam did not walk in this level of accuracy because of his closeness to God; it was simply because of his prophetic gift. There is a distinct difference between Balaam, in comparison to someone like Abraham. In Genesis 18:17, right before God was about to destroy Sodom and Gomorrah, He did something profound. He asked Himself a question, saying, "Shall I hide from Abraham what I am doing?". To me, this is one of the most intimate questions in the Bible. God is about to move and act, and instead of hiding what He is going to do, He chooses one man and shares with him what is in His heart. God shared His secret with Abraham because Abraham was His friend. God walked so intimately with Abraham where He, in a sense felt as though He would be betraying His relationship with Abraham if He did not share with Him the secrets of His heart.

Balaam could prophesy accurate words, yet he was different from Abraham. Both had prophetic callings, yet they differed because Balaam prophesied from gifting, whereas Abraham prophesied from a place of friendship. There is a very notable difference. Friends are the ones who are entrusted with the deep secrets of God's heart.

Amos 3:7 says, "Surely the Lord God does nothing, unless He reveals His secret to His servants the prophets." God has no obligation to share His secrets with prophets. Yet, He shares His secrets with the prophets because they are His friends. This should essentially be the goal of the prophetic ministry. It is getting so close to the Lord in friendship, that if He is going to act and move, He will share with you what He is going to do first.

People often ask me, "What is the key to moving in the anointing?" I think we can see an answer to that question in 1 Samuel 3:19. This verse talks about how God would not let any of Samuel's words fall to the ground. I believe this was because of Samuel's closeness with the Lord.

Have you ever noticed that when specific people ask Holy Spirit to show up in His manifest presence, God really shows up? The reason is because they are God's friend, so when they ask Him to do something, He does it. He does not let their words drop to the ground because He places weight on what they say due to their closeness in relationship.

A while back, I was invited to speak at a small church for their third year anniversary. For whatever reason, as I was speaking, I felt as though I was having an "off" day. Don't get me wrong, God was still moving. People were getting miraculously healed and set free. However, as I spoke I was constantly fumbling over my words and was forgetting key Bible verses, which I knew by heart.

At the end of the service, I was going to finish by getting everyone to stand, to pray a final release of healing. After everyone stood up, out of seemingly nowhere the presence of God poured out powerfully. Now, keep in mind that this is a church that is not used to experiencing the supernatural things of God. The few healings that they saw previously in the meeting was a huge stretch for them already.

However, for the next hour everyone was hysterically weeping in the presence of God. You could hear demons audibly shrieking out of people, and many were being healed right, left and centre. The entire place was in full blown kingdom culture.

Once the service had ended, I was clearly very satisfied with how the Lord moved. However, I was also perplexed since I did not minister as well as I normally do. As I spent time with Holy Spirit later that evening, I said to Him, "Lord, I love how you manifested Yourself today. However, why did you come so powerfully considering that I didn't do as well as I normally do?"

Holy Spirit then responded to me saying something that revolutionized how I understood moving in the anointing. He said, "I do not let My friend's words drop to the ground. Since you are my friend, I will always act on your behalf."

Isaiah 64:4: "For since the beginning of the world men have not heard nor perceived by the ear, Nor has the eye seen any God besides You, Who acts for the one who waits for Him."

A while back, I had a vision from the Lord that made me aware of something that is profoundly on His heart in this time. In this vision, I saw myself in a court room in heaven (Daniel 7). Around me in the courtroom were hundreds of thousands of people, Kingdom leaders, from throughout the world who were believing for a global move of God. Each of us looked around to one another in wonder as to why we were summoned to this particular meeting in the courts of heaven.

Suddenly, Jesus stepped onto the stage before us. He carried so much authority, that His very presence demanded the silence of hundreds of thousands of leaders. He is indeed the King of kings. He stood quietly for a time. Then suddenly He reached behind His back and pulled something forth. What He now held out in front of us to see was a mantle. As thousands of eyes watched Him, Jesus spoke, saying, "This was the mantle of a great man of God who led thousands of people into the Kingdom of God in his lifetime." Jesus said the man's name and went on sharing with us all of the great feats that this man had accomplished for the Gospel while he was on the earth. He truly honoured the man. Then Jesus said something which caught us all off guard. He said, "However, this man only completed 80% of the ministry that I had laid out before Him."

When Jesus said this, everyone who listened held their breath, waiting for what He was going to say next. Allowing silence to linger for a time, Jesus then finished what He wanted to say. He said, "The reason why this man only completed 80% of his ministry on the earth, is because he had forgotten his First Love. Since He did not put intimacy and friendship with the Godhead as his primary priority, he did not complete the mandate over his life.

Everyone looked at one another, wondering why Jesus was sharing information such as this. Jesus then continued, "Since My word cannot come back void, who here is willing to pick up this mantle to complete his mandate?" Silence reigned in the atmosphere for a time, when a woman stepped up to the stage and allowed Jesus to place the mantle on her shoulders.

When she left the stage, Jesus pulled another mantle out from behind His back. He said, "This was the mantle of a great woman of God, who led hundreds into the kingdom of heaven in her lifetime. Yet, she only completed 20% of her ministry because she forgot her First Love. My word cannot come back void, so who will pick up her mantle?" We waited again in silence until someone came up to take on the incomplete mandate. Jesus did this with dozens of mantles throughout the course of this meeting.

After my vision, Holy Spirit then spoke to me saying, "The most important test that any Believer will face in their lifetime is this question, 'Do you remember your First Love?'"

John 13:23-26: "Now there was leaning on Jesus' bosom one of His disciples, whom Jesus loved (John). Simon Peter therefore motioned to him to ask who it was of whom He spoke. Then, leaning back on Jesus' breast, he said to Him, 'Lord, who is it?' Jesus answered, 'It is he to whom I shall give a piece of bread when I have dipped it.' And having dipped the bread, He gave it to Judas Iscariot, the son of Simon."

This portion of scripture moves me deeply. I do not believe that it was only John who had this access to Jesus where he could lay his head on Jesus' chest to hear the secrets of His heart. I believe all of the disciples had the choice to be this intimate with Him. John simply made the decision to walk out the revelation in knowing that Jesus desired a deep love relationship with him. John, being the author of this gospel even calls himself "the one whom Jesus loved" (John 21:20). He did not write this out of pride, but was simply stating truth because he had a deep revelation that Jesus loved him just the way that he was. John did not have to wait until he walked in complete maturity before he could know Jesus like this. It was knowing Jesus this intimately that made him mature. Since John knew that Jesus adored him, he had the confidence to ask Jesus secrets and expect an answer back. This is probably why God trusted John to receive the important and heavenly secrets that were recorded in the book of Revelation.

Cultivating A Prophetic Lifestyle

I believe that God is raising up a "John the Beloved" generation. He is raising up a generation whose greatest desire will be to know Him. He is calling His people into the secret place to walk in intimacy with Him. Friendship with God is the greatest level of ministry, and God is looking for those who will first and foremost pursue the deep things of His heart.

We are living in amazing times, where God is birthing revival throughout the nations. Signs, wonders, miracles and salvations are happening all over the world. The only way for us to steward this move of God that is sweeping the earth is for us to prioritize our friendship with God above all else. This is where true love-filled authority is forged. It is forged in the face-to-face encounters with the living God. God is calling us all to prioritize our lives properly, that we may know Him, and as the by-product of knowing Him, complete the full mandate that is over our lives.

God is looking for a prophetic people who will not be content with simply prophesying. God is looking for friends, who He can share the deep secrets of His heart with.

Conclusion

As the bride of Christ, we are walking into a deeper understanding of intimacy and friendship with God. Since this is the case, Holy Spirit has been broadening my understanding in how prophets should be training the church concerning hearing the voice of the Lord. Prophets should not only be teaching how to prophesy; they should be training the church to operate in the mind of Christ wherever they are called.

The prophet Daniel was an incredible leader in government who served king Nebuchadnezzar. Nebuchadnezzar was the pioneer of a genocide. He created an enormous statue made of gold and commanded people to worship it. Those who did not were executed. Daniel, having favour with the king would speak the word of the Lord to him, not to empower his bad works, but instead to turn the king to God, thus bringing Babylon under God's blessing. It is interesting to note that Daniel was never once called a prophet throughout the entire book of Daniel. He was actually known by the king as the chief of the magicians. Daniel was the leader of all the mystics and magicians. He was an undercover prophetic leader who would speak the word of the Lord in his sphere of influence to steer the governmental ship right into the hand of God.

Since we are learning to tap into the mind of Christ, I believe that we are about to see the kingdom of God penetrating every vein of culture and society. We are entering into a time where the church is going to take the lead in business, government, media, arts, entertainment, education and family, for the expansion of the kingdom of God. I believe that we will do this when we learn to have vision to expand the kingdom of God wherever we are. We will be a people who are constantly in tune with the voice of Holy Spirit, because intimacy and friendship has bound us to that depth of fellowship with Him.

The prophetic community is not called to be bound within the four walls of the church. We are called to be "Daniels" to the marketplace. We are called as undercover prophetic people, who will release the word of the Lord through our different expressions of life. Prophecy needs to be bound to

Conclusion

integrity because the church is about to capture the eyes and ears of the nations.

Understand that you are not disqualified in any way or form from moving in the things of God, or from bringing healing to the world. Many in the church have disqualified themselves from being used by God because they have allowed their current or past circumstances to dictate how much of an impact they can make for God. Scripture shows us how many of Jesus' disciples rejected Him right before He was crucified. Two of the most well-known disciples who rejected Jesus were Peter and Judas. When faced with the possibility of persecution, Peter denied Jesus three times (Matthew 26:69-75). Judas, out of greed in his heart, gave Jesus up to be crucified (Luke 22:47-48).

There is something here I want to point out to you. Since Peter had a revelation of Jesus' grace, when he rejected Christ, he did not consider himself disqualified from the kingdom of God. Even though Peter blatantly rejected Jesus, Jesus simply restored Peter as a man, and as a leader. In fact, Jesus made Peter the leading apostle of the 12. Judas' response when he rejected Jesus was very different. When Judas sinned against the Son of Man, he disqualified himself within his heart from ever being used for the purposes of God, therefore committing suicide by hanging himself on a tree (Matthew 27:5). It is interesting that Judas hung himself on a tree. This gives us a powerful prophetic picture of how Judas did not believe that Jesus hanging and dying on the cross (a tree) for his sin was enough for him to be redeemed, so therefore in a sense, he crucified himself for his sin.

Unfortunately, this is a viewpoint where many in the church live their lives from. Due to our current or past circumstances, in our hearts we disqualify ourselves from being used by God. We therefore submit to a form of spiritual death, by believing that we are not worth being used. Realistically, we need to understand that Jesus would have treated Judas in the same regard as He treated Peter. I truly believe in my heart that if Judas was repentant and understood the power of the cross, Jesus simply would have restored him as a man and as a leader. I believe that it was God's will to restore Judas to a place of wholeness.

My friend, if you have ever felt like the last choice, then you are the perfect candidate to do remarkable things. God has a reputation for picking those who feel like they are nothing. He picks them, befriends them, and turns them into someone powerful. He is there for us throughout the whole story of our lives. He chooses us in our weakness and refines us to be strong in Him. He calls us when we are dependent on ourselves and others, and teaches us to be dependent on Him. I am so thankful that God chose Peter, the coward, and turned him into Peter, the apostle. I am so thankful that God called Matthew, the tax collector, and turned him into an apostle and

Conclusion

author of one of the gospels. God chose Moses, the murderer, and turned him into a man who delivered a nation. God chose David, the adulterer, and made him one of the greatest kings who ever lived. God chooses the least likely and uses them to do remarkable things (1 Corinthians 1:27).

While journeying throughout this book, some of you may have received an impartation on how to hear and speak the word of the Lord. Others may have learned about what the heart of God is through prophecy. No matter what you have received while reading, I want to end this book with a commission.

No matter who you are, or wherever you are called, God has called you to be His mouthpiece on the earth. Whether you are speaking to your children, to those on the streets, or to kings and government leaders, He has called you to release a royal decree within your sphere of influence. This royal decree is the message of the love of God. You are a son or daughter with a message of the Father's heart. You are a king or queen with a message of Christ's reign on the earth. You are a co-labourer with Christ, carrying a message of Holy Spirit's sweep of revival, which is riding throughout the nations. Now is your time to speak. Now is your time to reveal destinies. Your voice is important. It is not meant to be pushed down, but instead to be sounded like a victorious trumpet. Your voice is the vehicle for God's word, which will unlock hearts from bondage and into blissful freedom. God has chosen you to be an encounter to everyone you come in contact with. Now is the time for you to unashamedly share the love that you have received in your heart.

He who has ears let him hear. He who has eyes let him see.

Made in the USA
Charleston, SC
26 October 2016